BILL HYBELS

Just Walk Across the Room

SIMPLE STEPS POINTING PEOPLE TO FAITH

ZONDERVAN®

WILLOW
Willow Creek Resources

ZONDERVAN.com/
AUTHORTRACKER
follow your favorite authors

Just Walk Across the Room
Copyright © 2006 by Bill Hybels

This title is also available in a Zondervan audio edition.
Visit www.zondervan.fm.

Requests for information should be addressed to:

Zondervan, *Grand Rapids, Michigan 49530*

ISBN 978-0-310-27218-2

International Trade Paper Edition

Interior design by Beth Shagene

Printed in the United States of America

10 11 12 13 14 • 29 28 27 26 25 24 23 22 21 20 19 18 17 16 15 14 13 12 11 10

When Bill speaks, I listen. When he writes, I read. He has a unique blend of loving leadership. Heed his words!

MAX LUCADO
Author and Senior Minister,
Oak Hills Church

Bill has lived his life for the sake of people who need to know the love of Christ. He has reordered his private life to involve and include lost people so that he can share the gospel with them. If you want to learn from one of the great soul-winners of our generation, read this.

JOHN C. MAXWELL
Founder INJOY Stewardship
and EQUIP

Bill Hybels is a gift of God to the Body of Christ. I am convinced that these basic steps are the tools needed for 21st-century evangelism.

REV. JAMES T. MEEKS
Senior Pastor,
Salem Baptist Church of Chicago

This book reshapes how we think of evangelism as something we "do" on occasion to something we naturally "are" every day."

DAN KIMBALL
Author,
The Emerging Church

Accept Bill's invitation to walk across the room and into an exciting adventure that could transform someone's entire life—and eternity.

LEE STROBEL
Author,
The Case for Christ and
The Case for a Creator

Bill calls all of us to action as witnesses for Christ our Lord. Read his book and listen and heed the Holy Spirit's promptings.

CHUCK COLSON
Founder and Chairman,
Prison Fellowship

To the South Haven Gang
Your life-giving spirits have done more
for my soul than you will ever know

•   •   •   •   •

Contents

· · · · •

Acknowledgments

* * * * •

I have never achieved anything of significance without the aid of a great team. This project was no exception. From the beginning Ashley Wiersma helped me develop and edit the manuscript. In addition she rode point on the small group curriculum and the video shoot that accompanies it. Her skill and passion for this material were a huge inspiration to me. Garry Poole unselfishly shared the discoveries of "living in 3D" as he was pioneering a new way of talking about neighborhood evangelism at Willow. Scott Bolinder and the Zondervan team consistently expressed a level of enthusiasm for this book that was infectious to everyone who got near it. Dozens of my friends opened up their lives and stories in this book and gave me permission to share them. It's a generous move I won't soon forget.

Introduction

. . . . .

Two summers ago I experienced a serendipitous collision of circumstances while on a boating trip off the Wisconsin coast of Lake Michigan. I was alone, my heart was in a posture of worship, and I had some time on my hands. I'd pulled into a tiny harbor, tied up the boat, and was tidying up the place before relaxing for the evening. After studying my boating charts to determine where I would sail the next day, I realized I was only ten miles from the campground where I'd invited Christ to come into my life as a teenager.

I had visited that same harbor on several occasions throughout the years, but for some divine reason on that particular day, I was prompted to go stand on the hillside where I'd first met Christ. The more I thought about it, the more the idea gained steam; so I decided to hunt down transportation to get there. After finding a phone booth, I placed a call to the only cab company in town. Surely they would make the twenty-mile round-trip for me.

The dispatcher on the other end of the phone wasn't about to budge. "Sir, it's too long of a drive out there," she regretted to tell me. "We just don't do that." I haggled with her and even threw more money into the equation, but as the minutes ticked by it became obvious to me that I wasn't getting any closer to my meaningful walk down memory lane.

"Do you know *anyone* who would be willing to make the trip?" I pleaded.

Then, with newfound optimism, she told me she did. She knew a guy who was down on his luck and would probably do *anything* for money. (Should have been my first clue.) If I were willing to take a chance with him, she'd pass along his number.

I've never been opposed to reasonable risk, so twenty-five minutes later, a thoroughly trashed Ford Explorer pulled into the marina parking lot. Its owner looked equally ragged—not surprising, given my phone call had jolted him from a dead sleep at four o'clock in the afternoon. If I were a betting man, I'd have put money on him having more tattoo-covered flesh than not, but nothing was going to eclipse the allure of the mission for me.

I climbed in, and as we headed out, I noticed that all the things that were supposed to stay still on a car in motion were moving, rattling, shaking, and threatening to fall off at any moment. Ironically, the things that were supposed to move wouldn't—such as the passenger window. But the guy was nice enough, and frankly I was just glad to finally be en route.

The fuel gauge was on empty, and when I suggested we stop to let me buy him some gas, the man was incredulous. "Really?" he asked. "No . . . I couldn't do that."

"Come on, I insist," I told him. "You're really helping me out here, and I'd like to return the favor." We eased into the station, and he hopped out to start the pump.

"Two bucks. That's what I'm putting in," he said, as if asking my permission.

"Oh, go ahead and go crazy," I hollered toward him. "Make it ten!" When he joked that in the six months he had owned the vehicle, it had never had a full tank, we agreed to fill the thing up.

Back on the road, he had this huge grin on his face. "Handles different with a full tank!"

"Just keep her on the road, my friend," I laughed.

A few minutes later, we arrived at the camp entrance, and he asked what he was supposed to do while I handled my business. I could tell he was a little unsure about why I had hired a stranger to drive me all the way out to a deserted campground.

"I need to run up ahead for a few minutes to take care of something," I explained. "Why don't you wait here in the car—I'll only be fifteen minutes or so, and then we'll head back." That must have seemed reasonable enough, because he gave me a quick nod as I opened the door to get out.

As soon as my feet hit the ground, I jogged away from the truck, quickly covering the three hundred yards or so to reach the exact place where I'd encountered grace for the first time. And as I slowed down to approach that little patch of real estate on the side of that hill, the sun beating down on my face, it all came rushing back to me. This was the spot!

·   ·   ·   ·   •

By age seventeen I had already packed a lot of living into life. Even then I knew enough to recognize that the accumulation of more toys, the desperate search for approval, and the ceaseless striving for success just weren't cutting it. My spiritual experience that night at camp wasn't prompted by someone delivering a stirring message or by someone asking me three deep questions. I met Christ because while walking from a mess-hall gathering back to my cabin one night, I was suddenly penetrated by a single verse of Scripture that I had memorized as a kid: "Not by works of righteousness which we have done, but according to God's mercy he saved us."

He saved *us.* He ... saved ... us.

Just after nine o'clock that night, the words I'd read so many times before hit me in a fresh way. Could it really be true that God cared enough about me that he would make provision to save me? Even *me?*

For the first time in my young life, I faced my biggest doubt head-on: *There is no way I could matter so much to God that he would make salvation available to me as a gift—free of charge.* To that point, everything about my existence could be summed up in two words: "Earn it." My father had built into me a monstrous work ethic and had reinforced my Earn-It mantra daily. "You *earn* every penny you make," he would tell me. "You *earn* your way into the starting lineup on the basketball team. You *earn* good grades. You *earn* it all. There is no free lunch!"

I have been trying my entire life to impress God, I remember thinking. *I've poured all my effort into proudly presenting my good deeds to him—my righteousness, my hard work, my striving.* But I felt skeptical all the while— would it ever be enough? Truthfully, I wondered if I would ever reach God's quota and be found acceptable by him.

On that night in eastern Wisconsin, the Holy Spirit imparted to me whatever presence of mind I needed to understand Titus 3:5, and I met Jesus Christ in an authentic way. I remember throwing open the doors of my heart to him in what at the time felt like some sort of amazing grace attack. I don't know about your faith journey, but I felt the impact of my salvation experience *physically*.

I had run immediately to my cabin to find my buddies, elated by my discovery and armed with a series of "Guys, did you know … ?" questions about the grace I'd just stumbled upon. Since lightbulbs had gone on for me, I felt certain that my friends were still in the dark.

"Yeah, yeah, Bill, we know all that," they assured me. "Just go to bed!"

In the dark, silent stillness of the cramped cabin, I thought to myself, *I just never got it until now.* And from that night to this day, I've never really gotten over the power of grace.

·   ·   ·   ·   •

With my not-so-professional driver waiting for me in his truck, I stood in that place a few more minutes and thanked the God of the universe for seeking me out. I thanked him for imprinting that extraordinary verse on my mind at that precise moment in my journey and for radically altering the hinges of history in my life. I thanked him for redirecting me from the business world to the church-work world and for blessing me with a Christian wife and two fantastic kids — now adults who love to serve God and his church.

As if all that weren't enough, he had also surrounded me with great friends, challenging issues to address, and a compelling vision to pursue. What grace!

My gratitude list seemed to go on forever as my mind flooded with God-given gifts I'd received since that night at camp. I looked down at my feet on that hill, brushing the tears away, and thought, *It all started right here. Thank you, Father! Thank you …*

Wondering if I'd lost my ride, I pulled myself together and jogged back to the parking lot. I've never been so relieved to see such a rundown vehicle. After I climbed into the aging Explorer, my driver fired up the engine, and we started the drive back to the marina.

Not two minutes into the trip, he looked over at me. "What was *that* all about?"

I glanced over at him as he stared at the road ahead. "Me standing on the hill over there?"

"Gotta admit it's a little weird," he said. "I thought you were going to meet someone here or something. But you went to all this trouble just to stand alone on the side of a hill. What's that all about?"

"You really want to know?" I asked. When he nodded, I told him that I wanted to come stand on the exact piece of land where I met God.

"Really." He disguised his cynicism well. "And how exactly does something like that happen?" he asked.

I went on to explain how I'd had the most powerful experience of my entire life on the side of that hill. I told him how I had grown up hearing about God and learning about church but that I'd been on a self-improvement plan for years, always hoping to set righteousness records to earn my way into God's good favor. "Everything changed for me on that hill—it's the place where I learned that all of what I was trying to achieve would never get me into a relationship with God."

My comments sat in the air for a few seconds as I waited for some response that would tell me to keep talking. Suddenly, he piped up. "Well … then how the hell do you?"

Relishing his candor, I told him that the way it happened to me was through a single verse of Scripture. "For me, it was in the book of Titus—Titus 3:5 to be exact, which says that Christ 'saved us, not because of righteous things we had done, but because of his mercy.'"

More silence. Then with a hint of awkwardness, "Well that's a mind-blower, isn't it?" It was more statement than question.

He then asked what I had done after that verse hit me so hard, and I explained to him the process I went through of opening my will and my heart to Christ, of asking him to forgive my sin, of imploring him to lead my life through his great gift of grace instead of through my own striving.

As I finished my story, I couldn't help but wonder where he stood with regard to spiritual matters. The silence that ensued was broken by his heartfelt words. "Look at me, though. I'm a loser. I'm just a loser. I mean, can something like that happen to someone like me?"

What a holy moment, I thought as I collected my thoughts. "First of all, you're not a loser," I assured him. "You're anything but a loser. You're so important to God that he's been pursuing you since the day you were born. And you can have the same relationship with God that I found in my late teen years. It can happen to you anytime, anywhere. If you accept his gift of grace, you will be made new, and he will guide your life for the rest of your days."

When we arrived back at the marina, I handed him a handsome sum of money and thanked him for his willingness to help me out. As he prepared to leave, he said, "I never would've guessed that today would turn out like it did. Thanks for saying what you said to me. You know, there's a pastor starting a new church right beside where I live. He keeps coming by my apartment, saying this church presents the gospel message in a new way and that I might actually like it. The pastor's a pretty good guy, I guess, but I've been too stubborn to go. This weekend, maybe I'll check it out."

.   .   .   .   ●

As I climbed aboard the boat in the early evening hours, I sat down and reflected on those ninety minutes. My mind was preoccupied with so many questions. *What was that all about, God? Why was I prompted to go visit the camp today of all days, after being in this harbor so many times before? Why did I persist when the cab company said no? Why did I agree to call a complete stranger to see if he would haul me across town? And why on earth did I get into a truck like that?*

My questions culminated with this idea: *Won't it be something if I make that young man's acquaintance on the other side!*

Whether the experience was about my own need to reflect on a powerful conversion experience or whether it was all about taking a walk across a marina parking lot and offering hope to someone down on his luck, I don't know. But one thing I've learned is that life's great moments evolve from simple acts of cooperation with God's mysterious promptings —nudges that always lean toward finding what's been lost and freeing what's been enslaved.

The adventure of collaborating with God involves bestowing the greatest gift a person can receive—the gift of amazing grace—on undeserving (and often unsuspecting) people like you and me.

PART I

The Single Greatest Gift

CHAPTER 1

The Ultimate Walk Across a Room

* * * * •

Ten thousand steps.

Roughly, that's the distance you travel sunrise to sunset, each and every day of your life. It adds up to about 115,000 miles in a lifetime — or more than four times around this big blue planet of ours.[1]

With that said, just one question: Are you using your steps wisely?

Assume the average distance across most rooms is twenty feet — about ten steps. The question I hope to answer is this: What if ten steps — just one one-thousandth of your daily average — could actually impact eternity?

If so, it might well change the way you walk.

The concept surfaced many months ago after I attended a lunch in a southern state. Hundreds of us representing a variety of ethnicities gathered in a hotel ballroom, and I sensed I was in for an interesting experience. As the rest of my table convened, I would discover that our diversity went beyond race to span age, background, profession, and religion.

The moderator delivered some opening remarks and asked everyone to spend a few minutes before lunch making introductions, revealing where we lived, what we did for work, and why we'd come to the event. As we went through the exercise, I spotted a large African-American gentleman seated across the table from me. During his turn, he introduced himself with a name that was clearly Muslim. Then, halfway through the program, he caught my eye across the table and, in the midst of bustling conversations and clinking silverware, mouthed the words, "I *love* your books!"

Reflexively, I swiveled my head around to see if perhaps a bona fide author had approached our table from behind. Finding no one there, I turned back, dumbfounded, pointed my finger toward my chest, and mouthed, "Me?"

Grinning, he said, "Yes! Let's talk after lunch."

Yeah—a dose of intrigue ran through my mind—*let's do that.*

The lunch progressed while I racked my brain, searching for a rational explanation for how this Muslim man had stumbled upon my distinctly Christian books.

Afterward, he waved me over and began fitting the puzzle pieces together. "I now understand that my comment was probably a little confusing because you assume I'm a Muslim," he said.

"I try *never* to assume anything in situations like these," I laughed, "but yeah, I'm a little curious."

As he related his story, my heart and mind awakened afresh to the power of personal evangelism. The insight God would give me after interacting with this man would shed new light for me on how the Holy Spirit moves in the lives of Christ-followers when they commit to staying in vibrant, dynamic fellowship with God. After the encounter, I spent weeks thinking about his comments and growing increasingly awestruck by my discoveries about what *must* occur in the lives of Christ-followers for them to lead lives of impact.

·   ·   ·   ·   •

My tablemate had been a Muslim most of his life. He pointed out that being an African-American Muslim in a southern city, coupled with his current line of work, made for an often-uncomfortable existence.

"It hasn't been an easy go," he said. "As you might imagine, I've had a lot of struggles in social settings. And in my profession we have a lot of cocktail parties and other evening events. The natural pattern for me is to show up fashionably late, graciously accept a drink and something to eat, and throw my efforts into trying to make some business connections. Inevitably, I wind up standing alone, stuck against a wall or isolated in a corner. As soon as I think I've lasted as long as social etiquette requires, I discretely plot my exit and then leave. It's just something I've learned to live with.

"One night, I was at this type of party. As usual, I noticed several small circles of people forming to chat about this or that. I wasn't included, but again, I've become accustomed to the scenario.

"At one point, I saw a man on the other side of the room engrossed in discussion with a few people of his own kind, if you will. Suddenly he looked away from that particular group and noticed me standing alone by the far wall. This is exactly how it happened, Bill. He extricated himself from his conversational clique, walked clear across the room, stuck out his hand to me, and introduced himself.

"You know, it was so easy and so natural," the Muslim man continued. "In the moments that followed, we talked about our mutual profession, about our families and business and sports. Eventually our conversation found its way to issues of faith. I took a risk in telling him that I was Muslim —I was a little hesitant about how he'd respond. He told me he was a Christ-follower but that, truth be told, he knew almost nothing about Islam. You can imagine my surprise when he asked if I would do him the *courtesy* of explaining the basics of Islam over a cup of coffee sometime. Can you believe that? He said he was a curious type and genuinely wanted to understand my faith system and why I'd devoted my life to it.

"The next time we met, whatever doubts I had about him truly wanting to hear my beliefs were quickly dispelled. He *really* sought to understand my life and faith. We began meeting almost weekly, and each time I sat across from him, I was stunned by what an engaged and compassionate listener he was.

"One week, I even took the opportunity to ask him about his beliefs. I'd been a Christian as a kid but had left God, left the faith, left it all because the church my family attended was so racially prejudiced. I wanted no part of *that* Christianity. When the tables turned and I was on the receiving end of *his* faith story, he patiently described why he'd given his whole life to this person named Jesus Christ. I couldn't believe how easily the conversations evolved—and how respectfully and sensitively he conveyed his love of God. Despite our deep-seated religious differences, we were becoming fast friends.

"It went on this way for some time as we'd meet to hash through nuances of our faith experiences. Sometimes he would ask for a couple of days to find answers to my questions; other times, he knew exactly where I was struggling and seemed to have the perfect words to untangle my confusion. There finally came a day—I remember being home alone when this happened—that I felt totally compelled to pray to God. I kneeled beside my bed, told God everything I was feeling, and in the end gave my life to Jesus Christ. And in the space of about a week, that single decision changed *everything* in my world! Every single thing."

.   .   .   .   •

My heart was so full as his testimony washed over me. What a gripping story! I discovered that he'd recently become part of the leadership in his local church, which is where he had come across some of my books. And his steps of faith had already impacted his family, several of whom had begun making strides toward Christ. He really had begun a completely new life—one immersed in the companionship, power, and saving grace of Jesus Christ.

As I stood in the emptying ballroom of a sterile hotel on a muggy afternoon in the Deep South, I held my own private worship service, thanking God for redeeming this man, thanking God for changing his forever and for changing, very likely, the forevers of his immediate family.

All because of one man's walk across the room.

ENTERING THE ZONE OF THE UNKNOWN

Friends, I must hear a dozen salvation stories a week while traveling and ministering on behalf of Willow Creek. They come in various forms from all sorts of men, women, and children, and I celebrate each and every one of them! But on that day, as I sat on the airplane flying me to the next city, an interesting thought raced through my mind, warranting special reflection: *What if redirecting a person's forever really is as simple as walking across a room?*

There was something about that story that God wanted to sear into me, and it dealt with far more than the end result of a man coming to faith in Christ. It was as if God himself said, "If you'll invest some energy thinking about this story, I'll give you an image that will fire you up for a long, long time."

And as I mulled it over, what came into focus was a clear picture of what things must have been like for the Christ-follower during that cocktail party. He'd found himself in a social setting, engaged in what I have always deemed to be a "circle of conversational comfort." He was involved with a group in which it was easy for him to relate and effortless for him to engage. There was zero threat of anything risky or unsafe unfolding, which is why he had every reason to stay within the boundaries of that little Circle of Comfort, a place we've all enjoyed on one occasion or another.

Yet drawn by the fact that one man stood unintentionally and uncomfortably alone, he left that circle and walked stride by stride across the room. It was as though in a flash of insight, he heard a word of encouragement directly from the Holy Spirit: "Why don't you go over and extend a hand of friendship to that guy? Go see if he may need a little conversation or encouragement—who knows what might happen?"

As I chewed on the thought, I realized that not only did he see something and hear something as the Spirit guided him; he also *felt* something worthy of acting upon. The Spirit living inside him caused him to feel such compassion for the man standing alone that he excused himself from his Circle of Comfort, made the turn to the other side of the room, and started walking in the direction of a place I call the "Zone of the Unknown."

It's foreign territory, this zone. He had no clue what would happen when he stuck out his hand to the tall Muslim man. He knew nothing about where the conversation would go or if there would be any conversation at all. He was uncertain what this individual's reaction to him would be. But he was already committed. He had left his Circle of Comfort, he had walked by faith all the way across the room, and he had resolved in his heart, probably praying every step of the way, to enter into the Zone of the Unknown and see what God might do. (In my opinion, it's within this zone that God does his very *best* work.)

I couldn't think of another life-change story that had had as much impact on me. *But why?* I kept pestering God. *What is it about this one?*

The power of it, I concluded, was that it gave me a framework for something I'd been thinking about since my own salvation experience more than thirty years earlier: personal evangelism really *can* be as simple as a walk across a room—just a few ordinary Spirit-guided steps can have truly extraordinary outcomes.

CHRIST'S WALK ACROSS THE ROOM

There was an intriguing subplot to what God was revealing. It's as if he were saying to me, "*Now* you grasp with a fresh grip what my Son did."

Track with me along metaphorical lines, and I think you'll agree that the original (and consummate) work of personal evangelism began with a walk across a "room"—a very large room, in fact. At a certain point in history, Jesus Christ himself left the marvelous fellowship of the Trinity and the worship and adoration of the angels; he wrapped himself in human flesh, and he walked across the cosmos in order to stretch out a hand to people like you and me—many of whom were right in the middle of wrecking their lives.

Romans 5:8 summarizes Christ's redemptive strides: it was when we were helplessly in the throes of sin that Christ extracted himself from the *ultimate* Circle of Comfort—heaven itself—to step across time and space to rescue us. Jesus took a decided step toward the ungodly, embracing the worst this planet had to offer with acceptance and love and forgiveness. Miraculously, Christ's death for rebellious and sin-scarred people declared amnesty for *everyone*.

Think about it: giving your life for a noble person is one thing, but laying it all down for vagrants like us? It was an undeserved and unexpected move, to say the least. And the correlation is revolutionary to Christ-followers: we take walks across rooms because *he* took the ultimate walk across a room.

If you've ever wondered why God would go to such lengths to prove his love, you're in good company. To clear up any confusion his first-century audience might have had about why he came, Christ said, "I came to seek and to save what was lost."

That's it. *People* were Jesus' One Thing. And they still are. People who are sick. People who are lonely. People who are wandering, depressed, and hopeless. People who have gotten themselves tangled up in suffocating habits and destructive relationships.

I think of the story from John 8 when Christ appears in the temple courts, all set to teach the crowd that has gathered there. A group of Pharisees arrive on the scene, dragging with them a woman with a checkered moral past who's just been caught in the act of adultery. Imagine the horror of being thrust into such a public place, your worst sins on display for the masses to see. Adultery is a serious offense, the Pharisees argue, and in keeping with God's Law from the days of Moses, Jesus will surely agree to have this woman stoned to death because of her ghastly sin.

The Pharisees know that Jesus is in a bind, and you sense from the text that they enjoy, with a sort of morbid delight, forcing the self-proclaimed Messiah into the middle of a moral dilemma: If he lets the woman off the hook, he'll be denying the validity of the law. But if he allows her to be stoned, he might be accused of being unmerciful—or even of being an enemy of the Roman government, which was the only group allowed to carry out capital punishment.

Jesus' reaction is fascinating. "I assume you're going to stone her," he begins. "So if that's true, then let's at least bring some order to the process. Go ahead and stone her, but let's just form a line, and those of you with *no* sin, you get to be at the front of the line. You throw your rocks first."

Obviously, Christ's plan wrecks the Pharisees' whole day. And understandably, the law-loving Pharisees have no reply. One by one, their rocks thump to the sand and they walk away.

Jesus finds himself alone with this woman who has tasted forgiveness and mercy for the first time. Although he has every right to get in her face and criticize her poor life choices, the Bible says he chooses a different course. His travel-weary knees softly creak as he crouches down beside her, his eyes wet with tears. "I don't condemn you—really. That's not why I came. I came to redeem your failures, not to punish you for your mistakes. Now go—don't sin anymore. Start living a brand-new life today! Don't fall back into your same sinful habits. I will help you live a new life starting right here, right now."

Friends, is there a better picture of God's heart than this—the heart that invites someone to freedom instead of indictment? Without excusing the woman's sinful indiscretions, Jesus said, "Everyone has taken some wrong turns. Everyone is in need of forgiveness and redemption and healing. Everyone needs to know the love that only my Father can provide. *That* is why I've come." And with customary tenacity, he left the temple courts that day, unwavering in his belief that his restorative vision would one day be reality.

Still today, as you love people, serve people, point people toward faith in Christ, redirect wayward people, restore broken people, and develop people into the peak of their spiritual potential, you reaffirm your understanding of your primary mission in the world.

TUNING IN TO HEAVEN

Several years ago, I was copiloting a private aircraft that was headed back to Chicago from the West Coast. Piloting the plane was a gentleman I'd flown with several times before. On each occasion, once we reached cruising altitude and switched on the autopilot, we'd enjoy open conversations about any number of issues.

On that particular night, our dialogue was generally about the task at hand. We discussed flight patterns and weather conditions and altitude assessments, mostly prompted by air traffic controllers on the ground who were feeding updates to us. But with about ninety minutes left in the flight, I silently pleaded for God's intervention. *Help me direct things to more substantive issues.*

After the next intercom update, I ventured into the Zone of the Unknown and asked my pilot friend if he would ever make a flight like this without listening to air traffic control. Would he ever consider—even for a moment—silencing the radio and directing the flight alone?

He didn't waste any time answering. "Of course not!" he laughed. "It'd be crazy—I need all the information and assistance I can get my hands on ... especially in dicey weather."

I prayed for a boost of confidence and then said, "If you can believe it, some people fly through their entire life with the radio to heaven turned off. They receive zero input from God. They get no guidance, no wisdom, and no counsel. A lot of times, they fly blindly into bad weather and end up crashing and burning. You'd be surprised how many people do that."

Silence crept through the cockpit as I waited and prayed.

A few seconds later, his voice now sobered, he said, "I guess that would be pretty stupid, wouldn't it?"

I conceded that there were probably better approaches to life and then sat there awestruck as a full hour of redemptive dialogue unfolded en route to Chicago. "Well, how do you turn the 'radio' on?" he had asked. And so, in the most straightforward language I could find, I told him.

·   ·   ·   ·   •

Several days later, I reflected on the boldness I'd exhibited during that flight. I haven't always been so daring, but as I gave it some thought, I landed on an explanation for why it seemed to be showing up more often: I *really* believe the saving message of Jesus Christ. I don't only preach it; I believe it! I honestly believe that every wayward person I know would live a vastly better life if God's love, grace, and redemption were operating in their lives.

Do you believe this too? A man once told me that he never shares his faith with anyone. I thought it was an interesting comment and probed a little as to why he was so resolved about his role (or lack thereof) in evangelism.

His answer shocked me. "I would never want to inflict the burden of God on anyone," he said.

Wow. That is not at all the God I know, I thought. The God I know invaded my world with love, acceptance, and grace and stuck me on the back of a launched rocket at age seventeen that I still haven't peeled myself off of. Nor do I want to anytime soon!

But it's an interesting thought to ponder, isn't it: *Who is the God you know?*

Is the God you know full of grace and mercy and compassion? Is the God you know mysterious, surprising, captivating? Is he forever unchanging and yet always brand new? Does he inspire you with his big ideas about how your life can really count? Is he faithful?

In my experience, the people who find themselves taking walks across rooms have first landed on the belief that the God they know is *worth* knowing! They have cultivated a heart posture that says, "Well, of course everyone I know would want this type of relationship with God! I'm absolutely sure you'd all love what I'm experiencing here...."

If you are in love with the God you know, let me ask you to rewind your faith journey a little to your pre-Christian days. Recall that time in your life when you would get up in the morning and realize once again that you had nobody to share your day with. *Guess I'm doing this one alone too*, you'd think. Or you would drive to work and be the only one in your car. You'd have long stretches of time with no words from heaven and nothing supernatural invading your ho-hum world. You would violate your conscience and have zero awareness that grace could actually cover it, if only you'd ask.

Friends, if you have been wrecked by God's gift of new life—as I thankfully have—and if you want to live your life as an expression of love for the great God you know, then let's crank up our boldness meters and introduce as many people as possible to the God who wants desperately to enfold them in his grace!

THE GREATEST GIFT

My belief system hasn't always been so firm, but when I was in my early twenties and a student at Trinity College, my professor Dr. Gilbert Bilezikian delivered lessons that inspired me, convicted me, and compelled me to action. To a group of us who were leading a high school ministry at the time, Dr. B said, "Throughout the course of your life, you're going to give your life to something. You will. *All* people do. They give their lives to pleasure or to possessions, to the attainment of popularity or to the acquisition of more power. But always to something."

As he plowed ahead, I got sidelined by my own questions. What was I giving my life to? What was the one great *something* I was living for? I began to wonder whether I was really as concerned about other people as I said I was or if I was just hiding my self-interest behind a facade of interest. My heart shuddered as I stared at the truth about what captivated most of my thoughts. It wasn't exactly laudable.

During that season of life, I had been anticipating a lucrative career in business. But as Dr. B's words crept deeper into my heart, I was suddenly and powerfully drawn to one prevailing preoccupation—people. People who face a Christless eternity. People who are ostracized and isolated and hopeless. People who are living for achievements that do not fulfill, accolades that never satisfy, and money that doesn't bring genuine happiness.

I wanted to approach life like Jesus had. The mind of Christ hadn't been consumed by business gains or money or fame but instead was endlessly focused on one thing: people—those who were lost and found, young and old, rich and poor, sought-after and rejected. Never has anyone displayed such a prodigious obsession with people as did Jesus. And in his customarily straightforward style, Dr. B reminded me that Jesus' expectation is that his followers *share* this magnificent obsession.

"True followers of Christ who really get it right," he said, "give themselves to *people*. Most importantly, they give themselves to pointing people to faith in Christ. That is the highest and best use of a human life—to have it serve as a signpost that points people toward God." Dr. B summed up my entire belief system with a brilliant flash of insight: if you really believe in the redeeming and transforming power of God's presence in a person's life, then the single greatest gift you can give someone is an explanation of how to be rightly connected to him.

It's as though Jesus is saying to his followers, "What I did as I walked across the cosmos all those years ago, I now want *you* to do. Every day, try to point every person you meet to me. Live as though you actually *believe* that your parent, your coworker, and your neighbor would be better off if they knew my Father—if they were on the receiving end of his counsel, his wisdom, and his guidance. Become walk-across-the-room people who follow my lead! Be people who are willing to seize every opportunity I give you—not motivated by guilt or fear or obligation, but just with an eye on me, a pliable heart, and a passion for my people."

These days, I recognize just how correct Dr. B was. Because when most people I talk to really think through their own faith journeys, they land on the fact that Christ wasn't the only one who took a walk to rescue them. Almost without exception, Christ-followers tell me that their faith stories involve someone somewhere who took a risk to walk across a room and to reflect the curiosity, kindness, and love of Christ. Someone somewhere made the decision to take the gift they'd been given and bestow it on them—at the time, a wayward soul living very far from God.

When you choose to live by faith instead of by sight, taking these walks, extending yourself, and exhibiting care to people who need to be enfolded in community, there is something a lot like Jesus going on in your mind and spirit. According to the apostle Paul, it was Jesus who, "being in the very nature God, did not consider equality with God something to be used to his advantage; rather, he made himself nothing by taking the very nature of a servant, being made in human likeness. And being found in appearance as a human being, he humbled himself by becoming obedient to death—even death on a cross!"[2]

Let me say it again: the single greatest gift you can give someone is an introduction to the God who asked his Son to go the unthinkable distance to redeem them. And when you allow your life's great preoccupation to be people, you'll find that when Christ asks you to take a walk across a street, into a restaurant, up a flight of stairs, through a locker room, wherever, you are ready! You're ready to leave your Circle of Comfort and follow his lead because you remember the fact that Jesus once crossed an entire universe to rescue you—the same Jesus who was known to enjoy deep community from time to time but who would consistently and unapologetically excuse himself from a Circle of Comfort and walk in the direction of someone he could direct toward the Father.

Today, to Christ-followers all over the planet, he says, "Reflect my love! And repeat my action."

TAKE A WALK!

When my son was in the fifth or sixth grade, he joined a soccer league. And although Todd was a talented athlete for his age, team sports were a little intimidating to him.

The man who served for the next three years as Todd's soccer coach was a businessman named Brian, a fantastic guy who really loved kids. Miraculously, he built hope and confidence into my otherwise-apprehensive son and actually sold Todd on the idea that he could be a terrific soccer player.

For three years I stood on the sidelines at almost every game. My wife, Lynne, my daughter, Shauna, and I cheered for Todd beside other parents who were rooting for their little guys, all of us engaging in the obnoxious hollering that families do at youth soccer matches. Afterward, we'd typically enjoy a few minutes of fellowship with other families that attended Willow.

One afternoon, Brian was in the center of the field after a long day, loading cones into his car so that he could head home. Just then, the Holy Spirit said, "Walk across the soccer field and help him, Hybels. Leave this safe little group, and go see if you can get to know Brian." I can replay the scene in my mind as if it happened yesterday.

As I put one foot in front of the other and headed toward where Brian stood, I tried to prepare myself for whatever might unfold once I opened my mouth. *Ought to be interesting.*

After introducing myself, we chatted about the kids on the team, about what line of work Brian was involved in, and eventually about my occupation. He wasn't too thrilled to discover that I was a pastor, but as weeks went by, he continued to engage in brief conversations with me after games or practices.

Each time we talked, I would thank Brian for the meaningful impact he was having on my son. "I appreciate how much time you volunteer out of your busy schedule to coach these kids," I would tell him. "I think what you are doing is noble and classy, Brian. I'll always be grateful."

On one day in particular, when we were nearing a holiday service at Willow, I was prompted by the Spirit to walk across that soccer field again, this time to see if Brian would like to attend the service. Mustering an additional ounce of courage with each step I took, I asked him if he would consider coming to Willow just once with me.

His response instantly erased any hope of receptivity on his part. "Oh, man, Bill, I *knew* it would turn into this! I just *knew* someday it would land here. Look, I know plenty about Willow Creek—I get tied up in its traffic every week. The whole thing frustrates me. God is not part of my life, church is not part of my life, and I'd just as soon take this whole thing off of the agenda here." (Hey, at least he was clear.)

"Okay, Brian," I said, trying to relax him. "No pressure, I promise. I'm committed to respecting your wishes."

And each week the following year, I would walk step by step across that soccer field to help him pick up balls and cones. How small those steps felt! Was I helping at all?

"How'd things go this week?" I'd ask. And we would talk about business and the deals he was working on. Then he would ask me how my week had been. I suppose my no-pressure approach served its purpose: I no longer offended Brian with unsolicited invitations to church. But to me, the whole experience seemed like an exercise in spiritual water-treading.

Eventually Todd cycled out of the soccer league, and I lost contact with Brian altogether. Frankly, I assumed I'd never see him again. But after several years had passed, the day came when Brian's world was turned dramatically upside down. Business issues shifted. His family life tilted. In sobering and unexpected ways, pain and despair walked through the front door of his life and took up residence there.

He picked up the phone and called me one afternoon to ask if he could come by to talk. "I *don't* want to come to a service," he clarified. "I just need to talk about a few things."

After that initial meeting in my office, Brian and I would meet several times, but I'd sense only minuscule progress during the conversations. At some point, he stopped calling altogether. And although I wondered how he was managing in life and whether or not he'd ironed out his pain, I honored his desire to lead the pace of our relationship.

Months later, I was standing at the front of the auditorium preparing a group of new believers for their upcoming baptism experience. As I explained the meaning, purpose, and significance of water baptism, I looked to my left and saw Brian sitting there, right in the front row. *He has no idea where he is!* I thought. *He's in a baptism meeting, for crying out loud. How did he stumble into this one?* I regained my composure long enough to finish my comments, being extraordinarily careful to complete my instructions in a way that wouldn't screen out a guy like Brian for the rest of his life. There was no way he was ready for the *baptism* deal!

After the meeting, I approached Brian and asked him to walk with me to the parking lot. "I've got to get going," I explained, "but let's at least talk on the way out." As soon as we had moved away from the crowds, I stopped and looked Brian right in the eyes. "What in the world were you doing in a baptism meeting?"

His answer floored me.

"A couple of months ago, I snuck in during a service and sat in the back. You were giving a message on abandoning the self-improvement plan and getting on board with the grace plan instead. You talked about the need to open ourselves to God by accepting the work of his Son, Jesus Christ. And on that day, Bill, I gave my heart to Christ. So what I'm saying is, I was here tonight—believe it or not—because I want to be *baptized.*"

His face was beaming as mine fell slack-jawed. I couldn't hide my astonishment. "You have *got* to be kidding me. Really. You have got to be kidding me!" I stood there staring at him with a dumbfounded look on my face for probably two full minutes.

Sometime after that conversation, I had the privilege of baptizing Brian at Willow Creek, the place where he still continues to serve, the place where he fell in love with a godly woman and was married, and the place where he and his wife now teach other couples how to experience the joy and elation of a Christ-centered marriage.

. . . . •

A few weeks before Christmas a couple of years ago, I was headed to my office with Todd, who was all grown up by then. We turned the corner in a stairwell, careening right into a large, muscular man. Instinctively, I took a step back as I looked up. It was Brian! And in a split second, a fifteen-year void between my son and his favorite childhood coach was filled. With the type of love that only Christ-followers can manifest, he threw his arms around Todd's neck. "How great it is to see you!" Brian raved.

After a few moments of conversation, Brian headed down the steps. When he reached the first landing, he stopped and looked up at us. "Hey, Bill," he said, "I just want to thank you for all those times you walked across the soccer field and opened yourself up. Really ... thanks." And with that, he turned to go.

Friends, that's as good as it gets in my world. And my guess is that similar experiences would qualify for your life's as-good-as-it-gets moments too. Knowing that the God of the universe has equipped you to bestow the greatest gift in this life on another human being, choose today to lead a life of impact—eternal impact.

Take a walk! See what he might do.

STUDY QUESTIONS

1. In the story of the Muslim man coming to faith in Christ, to whom do you relate the most: the Muslim man himself, the man who walked across the room at the cocktail party, or one of the people still standing in the "Circle of Comfort"? Why?

2. Romans 5:8 says that it was while we were sinners that Christ saved us. Why is it significant that he "walked across the cosmos" while we were still in our sin?

3. In John 8, when Christ encounters the woman who has been caught in adultery, he immediately reflects God's compassion, gentleness, and love. Does this picture mesh with who you know God to be? Why or why not?

4. On page 29, one of Christ's desires for all believers is stated this way:

   Live as though you actually *believe* that your parent, your coworker, and your neighbor would be better off if they knew my Father—if they were on the receiving end of his counsel, his wisdom, and his guidance. Become walk-across-the-room people who follow my lead! Be people who are willing to seize every opportunity I give you—not motivated by guilt or fear or obligation, but just with an eye on me, a pliable heart, and a passion for my people.

5. How would you rate yourself on the following items?

   TRUE   FALSE   I believe that every person I know would be better off living God's way.

   TRUE   FALSE   I live my life in such a way that others around me know I believe this.

   TRUE   FALSE   I want to become more of a walk-across-the-room man or woman who jumps all over evangelistic opportunities God lays in my path.

   TRUE   FALSE   I'm willing to let go of other passions so that God's people can take top priority.

CHAPTER 2

The Way to Sustain Evangelism

During the span of my adult life, I've witnessed dozens of evangelistic fads. Perhaps you can remember some of the eras I've seen rise and fall. Let's see, there was the Tract Era. The Televangelist Era. The Bus Ministry Era. There were eras revolving around saving professionals, saving women, saving men, saving the rich, the poor, homemakers, movie stars, you name it.

And to the extent that any of these approaches brought people to Christ, I am genuinely grateful.

But each time a new approach surfaced, I secretly wonder how long the wave would last, how long the movement could possibly be sustained. Sure, even I hopped on a few of them, but I knew they all lacked longevity.

In the next few decades, I'm quite certain there will be even more "new and exciting" approaches to evangelism. And I'll say it again: If people find faith as a result of them, who am I to criticize? But as far as I'm concerned, there is only one paradigm that will not wear thin with the passing of time. These days, I'm more convinced than ever that the absolute *highest* value in personal evangelism is staying attuned to and cooperative with the Holy Spirit.

You read it right. The only thing you need in order to sustain an effective approach to evangelism year after year after year is an ear fine-tuned to the promptings of the Holy Spirit.

SPIRIT-DIRECTED PROMPTINGS

Finding words to adequately define the promptings of the Holy Spirit is no easy feat. Promptings are mystical. They are phenomenal. They are intangible. And they're real. In fact, promptings have been present in the lives of Christ-followers since Jesus left his bodily form on earth and ascended to heaven. Remember? That was the day when he sent the Spirit of God to take up residence in the heart of every believer. "You will receive power when the Holy Spirit comes on you," he said. (It should clue us in to the challenging nature of our mission that Christ would need to send a permanent source of supernatural power to assist us.)

But what exactly was this power all about? The rest of the story from Acts 1:8 explains that Christ-followers have a mission while here on earth. They are to be Christ's witnesses all over this planet. It's as if Christ said, "Think you're missing the book smarts, the street smarts, the looks, the talent, or the speaking ability to accomplish this mission? Don't be concerned with those things, because you have my mountain-moving, life-transforming, death-defying power on your side."

In Galatians 5:25, Paul encourages Christ-followers to "keep in step with the Spirit." In other words, the Galatian believers should consider tapping into the power of God that is living right inside of them. This concept applies to you and me as well. If we have access to the vast power of the Spirit living inside of us, then why would we neglect to act on the guidance, motivation, and inspiration he offers?

I don't know about you, but when I am relating in a healthy manner with Jesus, there's vitality and openness in *my* spirit to the promptings of *his* Spirit. Staying attuned to the Spirit means I have a heightened awareness of the things going on around me. In the midst of a Circle of Comfort, I find myself able to keep one eye open and roving to watch for someone I'm supposed to see. I'm able to keep one ear open for the Spirit's whisper. Even though my spiritual senses are far from perfect, in those "attuned" moments, I am incredibly alert to God pointing me toward someone across a room, his gentle voice saying, "Just walk ..."

Every time I hear those two words, I'm reminded of what it's like to excuse myself from a Circle of Comfort. Of how electrifying it feels to make that turn and begin to walk, imploring God with every step for his intervention, his words, and his wisdom. Of the sensation of entering the Zone of the Unknown, each time as if in slow motion, putting my hand out there, and offering a few words of profundity: "Hi. I'm Bill. What's your name?"

And then of the sheer elation of watching God open a door in the other person's heart as the conversation meanders to spiritual matters.

Friends, although I have experienced a lot in life, been a lot of places, and engaged in my share of excitement, having a front-row seat when a person's heart gets transformed is what life in all its fullness looks like to me. To this day, when I am prompted to walk across a room, explore this Zone of the Unknown, and enter into these initial conversations with someone whose eternity is hanging in the balance, I experience a buzz that never, ever grows old.

*   *   *   *   ●

On the day of my conversion more than three decades ago, I was filled with an overwhelming hunger to share God's redemptive story with people who had never heard it. Unfortunately, I was committed to doing so with or without the accompanying direction and power of the Holy Spirit. (Details, details.)

But over the years, I trust that my increasing maturity has factored a little discernment into the equation. These days, I try to wake up each morning declaring, "My life is in *your* hands, God. Use me to point someone toward you today—I promise to cooperate in any way I can. If you want me to say a word for you today, I'll do that. If you want me to keep quiet but demonstrate love and servanthood, by your Spirit's power I will. I'm *fully* available to you today, so guide me by your Spirit."

Sometimes, the end result of praying this prayer is that the Spirit allows me to have a spiritual conversation that tells of a loving and righteous God who created all things, who has a purpose in mind for all people, and who is actually hoping to relate with them as they walk through life. Other times, the Spirit simply prompts me to serve and love and listen to the needs of those who are far from God. The key is this: my objective is not to contrive ways to "get someone saved"; rather, my objective is to walk when he prompts me to walk, talk when he says to talk, fall silent when I'm at risk of saying too much, and stay put when he leads me to stay put. If I can lay my head on the pillow at night knowing that I have cooperated with the promptings of the Spirit that day, I sleep like a baby.

If I'm serious about being transformed by God's Spirit, then I can't shy away from the discomfort and awkwardness and ambiguity that exist when I abandon my safe Circle of Comfort. The upside is too great to do that, because when I feel a Spirit-led prompting to walk across a room for the first time, it's like live voltage coursing through my veins. As I put one foot in front of the other to reach out to someone who may be twenty feet away from me but who's living light-years away from God, I'm part of something immeasurably greater than myself.

This is what it's like to experience God's supernatural power at work in an otherwise ordinary day. And the Bible says that this is what real living is all about—walking through *every* moment plugged into the Holy Spirit.

LETTING THE SPIRIT LEAD

One afternoon before I was to speak at our midweek service, I dropped into a local place to get a haircut. As I sat in my car outside of the shop, I said out loud, "God, if you want anything to happen in there—if you want me to say a word for you or try to help meet someone's need—then for the next twenty minutes or so, please know that my heart is ready. I'm completely available."

I walked in and was led by the receptionist to an open chair. I didn't know the woman who began cutting my hair, but there wasn't really time for introductions. She was hip-deep in a rapid-fire conversation with the hairdresser and client immediately to my right. It was unlike anything I'd ever witnessed. They covered everything from weather to culture to politics to Oprah in eight minutes flat. My eyes darted back and forth, watching conversation's form of Wimbledon unfold right before my eyes.

In my humble opinion, I had zero chance. Even acknowledging that they'd have to come up for air eventually, there was no way that I could wedge something into that conversation with any relational intelligence whatsoever.

Silently, I kept reminding God of my offer. *I really am open, God, but this conversation isn't! I sense no opening here, and if I try to shoehorn a Christian witness into this situation, I honestly think I'll do more harm than good.*

When she finished my haircut, I thanked her, gave her a tip, and told her that I sincerely appreciated her help, given how little she had to work with. With that, I walked out of the shop.

Now, based on the information I've given you, how do you think I felt after the experience was over? Disappointed or defeated, perhaps? Or maybe like I'd thrown a bad spiritual dice roll?

Believe it or not, I didn't. I was open to the movement of the Holy Spirit from the moment I walked in, and I sensed nothing that prompted me to probe, say, or do anything. I had been willing to see, hear, and feel what the Spirit wanted me to see, hear, and feel, but frankly I saw, heard, and felt ... *nothing*.

*   *   *   *   ●

Now contrast that occasion with a far different kind of experience. Frequently, I hide out in a particular restaurant to work on my talks, and for some time now, the same woman has been my server. She is an older woman with a daughter in her twenties. Based on my frequent conversations with her, I'd say that she is from another ethnic background and hails from a different part of the world, that she follows a completely different faith system, that she has never before darkened the doorstep of Willow, and that she probably has never heard a Christian witness in her life.

On this particular afternoon, I was preparing a talk for the upcoming Christmas Eve services. At one point I looked up, saw her across the restaurant as she was bussing a table, and was reminded of how faithfully and conscientiously she had served me each time I'd camped out there.

I heard the directive so clearly in my spirit that it may as well have been audible. *If she were to die anytime soon, she'd probably live apart from God for all of eternity,* he said. *Get up, walk across this room, and invite her to the Christmas Eve service. Just stand up and go talk to her!* So, as you'd expect from a spiritual heavyweight like me, I stayed seated and opted for debating with the Holy Spirit instead. *She's not going to come to a Christmas Eve service,* I pleaded silently. *She's got a whole different deal going on!*

You can guess who won that one. My mind was flooded with memories of the conversations she and I had shared over time, interspersed with a few convicting thoughts. *She knows who I am. She knows what I do for a living. And throughout all of our exchanges, I've been so careful not to badger her or "guilt" her into coming to church. Just this once I need to be bold.* After taking a deep breath, I approached her.

"You know, I've been very careful not to be a bother to you in a religious sort of way when I'm in here." Another deep breath. "But I'd like to invite you and your daughter to our Christmas Eve service. I think you'd enjoy it, but please know that I'm really not trying to mess with your mind and your faith. I just want to let you know you are welcome to come, and if you choose to, I can find a way to get you a few tickets." So I made a provision for her regarding the tickets, and I went back to my table, assuming she would not come.

Six weeks later, I walked in again, prepared to hash through some sermon work, and she immediately came up to me. "I *loved* your Christmas Eve service!" she blurted out. "I was there. My daughter was there, and she loved it too. It was the first time she had ever heard anything like that."

Then she dropped her key line on me: "I understood *everything* you talked about," she said. "I understood the whole service! I really want to thank you for inviting us."

After I picked myself up off the floor, I told her what an honor it was that she spent Christmas Eve with us. And once again, I considered God's providence. *How does this stuff happen?* I asked him. *What is this mystical ability of yours to draw people to yourself?* While I'll never fully understand it, it is a high privilege to be part of God's activity in the lives of his children.

Friends, sometimes there will be a wide-open door, and sometimes there won't. Remember, being walk-across-the-room people means that we walk when the Spirit tells us to walk, and we don't walk when the Spirit says not to. This dynamic is what makes the adventure mystical and unpredictable, exhilarating and God-driven. It is what keeps us on Christian life's exciting edge!

A DIFFERENT SPIN ON EVANGELISM

"But, Bill," you might be saying, "how can you possibly claim that the highest value in evangelism is something *other* than walking down the Roman Road or reciting the Four Spiritual Laws verbatim? Aren't we supposed to get a seeker to cross the finish line, seal the deal, and check the salvation box? Isn't the whole goal here to see people, uh, *come to faith in Christ*?"

I realize some of you believe that unless the plan of salvation gets explained, it's been an unsuccessful conversation, spiritually speaking. And some of you probably put yourselves through an exhaustive self-deprecation routine unless you extend an invitation to your church each time God opens an evangelistic door. Still others might say that everything is A-OK on your evangelistic value meter as long as you give your personal testimony—all four volumes of it—at every opportunity.

And I feel your pain! I can run myself through all these wringers with the best of them. But here's the reality: the Holy Spirit will bust your nice, neat evangelism formulas every time.

To be perfectly honest, I would love it if the work of evangelism were predictable. It would be marvelous if every single conversation I had with someone far from God led to a profession of faith. I would be the happiest person on the planet if every interaction I had with a seeker yielded a falling-on-the-knees experience. But you know as well as I do that real life paints a far different picture.

I've had to learn the hard way that on some occasions, the Spirit asks me to be an opener. I have a hoe, and I'm supposed to break up some really hard soil in someone's heart so that the next person to come along might have some influence in planting a seed or two along those rows.

On other occasions, the Spirit asks me to play the middle guy, carrying around a watering can and helping quench a few thirsty souls. Still other times, I'm supposed to pick really ripe fruit off the vine. I might describe it this way: I believe many people begin their spiritual quest at a negative ten and that my role is to facilitate their movement to a negative eight. That's it. Two points on the spectrum, and a result that is still in negative territory! It used to discourage me, but at some point I began to accept the fact that the role I am supposed to play is ... well, the role I'm supposed to play.

Likewise, the Spirit might prompt you to take someone who is standing at negative ten a few ticks forward to a whopping negative four. Or you might have the privilege of taking someone who is teetering right on the edge all the way to a positive one, right across the supernatural line of faith. The thrill of it all exists in the fact that as we walk into a spiritual exchange, you and I have no idea what role the Spirit has ordained for us to play.

SEED-SOWING FOOLS

Do you remember the parable of the seed that Jesus told? The story was told with the intention of explaining the various ways in which the good news of the kingdom will be received. One day, a farmer went out to scatter seed along the ground. Some of the seed fell on the road, and birds ate it. Some fell in the gravel; it sprouted quickly but couldn't put down deep roots, so when the sun came up it withered just as quickly. And some fell onto wild grass; unfortunately, just as it came up, it was strangled by thick weeds.

But the story didn't end there. Jesus went on to promise that despite where all of the other seed fell, *some* seed fell on good earth and produced a harvest beyond the farmer's wildest dreams. We cannot forget the reality of this fourth soil, friends. Jesus pledges to us that some of the seed we sow *will* fall on good soil.

Have you ever wondered why Jesus told this story? Personally, I think it was to give us a massive dose of evangelistic encouragement. What you and I experience in growing faint of heart is no different than what Jesus' disciples faced. After all, it's easy to get cynical when sowing seed. Surely the disciples had moments when they believed it was *all* falling on bad soil: "Here we are, trudging from town to town, and we just keep getting the stuffing kicked out of us," they must have said. "We leave uprisings in our wake. People hate us! There's not enough seed falling on good soil. We just don't see enough!" I'm sure if baseball existed back then, they would have howled that their batting average was way too low.

Jesus' response to them sobers me every time. In short, he said, "It's true, guys. You're going to walk across a lot of rooms, sow a lot of seed, and come away feeling fruitless. For any number of reasons, sometimes the soil just won't take the seed." He wasn't naive. Jesus Christ knew that fulfilling his redemptive mission would be excruciatingly difficult, risky, downright defeating, and seemingly fruitless at times. "But if you will just persevere," he might say, "the potential is colossal. Think of it! One more treasure—a priceless human being—might be snatched from the clutches of a horrendous, lifeless eternity because of your work. So go! Go right now and bear witness. Sow the seed. Take the walk across the room. Leave what's comfortable for that which is eternally significant. Risk your life for this, and know that you will never regret your decision."

He challenges us to do the same. "What does it profit a person," Jesus once said, "to gain the whole world but forfeit their soul?" (Mark 8:36). What Christ intended was for us to understand that we would be in eternity longer than we would be in this life. Our families will be in eternity longer than on earth. Our friends and neighbors and bosses—they will all be in eternity longer than on earth. "And you can play a role in redeeming them all!" Christ promises.

In short, "You *cannot* give up! Be seed-sowing fools, if you want to think of it that way, because someday—during one of those times when you risked taking a walk across a room—that seed is going to fall on the right soil, take root, germinate, and sprout. And you will fall to your knees in disbelief, saying, 'Thank God I did not give up! Thank God I did not flee to my little insular Circle of Comfort and stay there in hiding. Thank God *this* seed fell on good soil.' "

·   ·   ·   ·   •

Recently, I received a phone call from a staff member who reminded me that several years earlier he and I'd had a few interactions with a leader in the Chicagoland community who was admittedly pretty "me-focused" in his lifestyle. This gentleman never thought about spiritual things, he did not attend church regularly, and he really didn't have much use for God.

"Yeah, yeah, I remember him," I said as I thought back on those meetings.

"Well, he has had a few strains and stresses in his life in the last few months," the staff member explained. "He called me, and he would like to meet with us, Bill—you and me both. Can you swing that?"

My mind raced through the dozen things I had to do before flying off for an international trip. "I'm wall-to-wall meetings," I begged. "I'm just … if I had even five minutes, you know, I'd be happy to, but—"

"Bill," he interrupted, "would you mind just praying about it?"

There it was, the dirtiest trick in the book. *What am I supposed to do with that one?* I silently protested.

So I prayed about it. Honestly, I did. And not surprisingly, the Spirit told me that this meeting was something I should devote time to, even if it had to get wedged between weekend services—which it did. The staff member arranged the meeting, and on that blustery Sunday morning, the local leader joined us in my office for what turned out to be an anointed conversation.

After exchanging a few pleasantries, I took the risk to dive right in. The clock was ticking! I asked his permission to sketch out what most people think of Christianity versus what the Bible says is really true about it. He said that would be fine, so I continued.

"Most people think of Christianity as a scale. All of the bad things you've ever done sit on one side, and all of your good deeds sit on the other. In this scenario, life's *ultimate* goal becomes working to load as many good things as possible on your scale so that by the time you draw your final breath, things lean in the right direction. Most people think they'll wind up sitting pretty in the next world — if they even believe in a 'next world' — as long as they can get the scales tilted right."

I looked up to check for understanding.

The man said that I'd done a fair job representing his current view of Christianity, so I took things a step further.

"While this may *seem* right, the Bible teaches that this is not what life's about at all! God basically says that we could never tilt the scales enough to be found acceptable by him. But because he loves us so much, he didn't leave us without hope. God says that we can accept what his Son did in dying on a cross for our sin, paying for every bad deed we have ever committed and will ever commit. Then, by the power of his love, we'll be accepted by him and will spend all of eternity by his side."

I looked over my desk at him as he nodded in agreement. With a beat of trepidation stomping through my heart, I swallowed hard and asked, "Would there be any reason why you wouldn't want to ask Jesus Christ to forgive your sin and to become the strength and power and guide in your life, starting today?"

He looked up at me, the air in the room suddenly arrested.

"No ... I suppose there isn't," he said as we both exhaled. "Actually, I can't think of anything that would keep me from doing that!" So, fully enabled by the Spirit of God, I prayed the prayer of salvation, listening as he repeated each phrase. Later, I would baptize him and help him get involved in a small group where he could flourish in his newfound faith.

His amazing story is just one more example of the transforming love of Christ. But here's what intrigues me most about it: I put a grand total of *zero* effort into that relationship. I wasn't the guy who worked with him inch by inch from a negative ten to a negative seven. I was nowhere to be found the day he left negative three and found negative one. Other people besides me served faithfully as key influencers along this man's path, and I simply happened to be in the right place at the right time to welcome him into positive territory.

Sure, I tried to be prepared. I had half a dozen illustrations in my hip pocket so that I could respond appropriately to his specific needs. And as much as possible, I dialed in to the movement of the Holy Spirit so that I didn't botch my particular role that day. But in the end, my assignment was merely to show up, ask a simple question, and sprint beside this guy as he crossed the line of faith.

Someday, friends, there comes a harvest. Someday there is a payoff. Someday sinners become saints. And between now and then, we get to keep spreading the message. We get to keep playing the roles we are meant to play. We get to keep planting seeds, trusting that God will bring the increase. Because in due time — oh, the increase that he brings!

* * * * *

Possibly the most profound evidence of this seed-sowing approach "working" is found in the life of my buddy Tommy Giesler. Years ago, I started a sailboat racing team with nine other guys. Although all nine of them could have contended for the honor, Tommy took the prize for resident Wild Man. This fun-loving friend soaked up three years of my most earnest prayers. I used to have candid heart-to-hearts with God, telling him all the reasons Tommy would be a fantastic follower of his if God would just get his attention.

There were many times when after a long day of sailing, Tommy and I would stay up late talking about everything under the sun. On other occasions while out of town for sailing regattas, I played nursemaid to him after he'd had a little too much to drink. For three years I did this. I invested in Tommy for three years. I prayed for Tommy for three years. I loved Tommy for three entire years. (Did I mention this went on for three years?)

As you'd expect, despite our deep theological differences, Tommy and I had developed a solid friendship. I trusted the guy so much that one time

I arranged for him to take a group from Willow on a sailing trip, using a friend's boat. I couldn't make it, but I figured Tommy could handle things. A couple of days into the trip, it seemed all was well at sea. The sun was high, the waves were rising in a perfectly steady rhythm, and everybody was having a fantastic time.

That afternoon, a guy from Willow named John felt prompted to ask Tommy a spiritually directed question. He'd been talking with Tommy off and on for two days straight by that point and felt like it was a calculated risk. "You've been processing stuff with our senior pastor, right, Tommy? Talking about matters of faith and all that?"

A big smile burst onto Tommy's face. "Yeah, I've really enjoyed all the talks with Bill. It's been great!"

Tommy and John then dove into an incredibly deep and candid conversation, culminating with a rather bold question. "Hey, Tommy," John asked, "why wouldn't you just come across the line of faith right now and open up your heart to receive Jesus Christ?"

Tommy said that now that he thought about it, nothing was keeping him from doing something like that. All he needed to know was how to get things squared away.

So John said, "Well, all you need to do is pray to God ...," and John prayed right there with Tommy for him to receive Christ. According to John, who was studying Tommy's every move after the prayer was over, genuine conversion happened. "You could just tell," John said sometime later. "It was the real deal. The Holy Spirit really grabbed hold of this guy!"

A few minutes after this whole thing unfolded, I received a long-distance phone call from Tommy. "Bill! Guess what!" he shouted.

He had wrecked the boat; I just knew it. "You wrecked the boat; that's what," I ventured. "You went out and got hammered and wrecked the boat."

"No, no, no," Tommy said. "Listen. Your friend John helped me to give my life to Jesus today. I did it! I'm so excited, I had to let you know."

My silence was lost on Tommy, who was too elated to pay attention to me. Yeah, my *friend* John. Some friend! Three years I worked on this guy, and one day out of nowhere, John waltzes in, asks one question, and presto, Tommy's a believer! "Since when is *this* fair?!" I yelled toward the ceiling.

To this day, whenever I bump into John around Willow, I say the three words that make him chuckle every time: "*Still* not fair!"

The moral of the story is that we can't ordain the role we get to play, and we certainly can't predict the time frame of someone coming to faith. The Spirit of the holy, omnipotent, omnipresent God gets to play that part. And it's a marvelous system, if you really think about it.

Take the situation with Tommy. I'll never know if John could have moved Tommy from negative six to negative five. But I believe the Spirit used me to do so. And I'll never know if there would have been an opportune time for me to help Tommy cross the line of faith into positive territory. But guess what? The perfect moment *did* come for John, and he seized it. I believe we both played the roles we were intended to play. Nothing more, nothing less.

As you go about your days playing only the role you're prompted to play, you too will participate in the wild mystery of it all. And every role is a valid one — Acts 24 reflects this truth well. As the story unfolds, it's clear that the apostle Paul had been falsely accused yet again, finding himself cross-legged on the cold floor of a prison cell, keenly aware that he could be wrongfully convicted and put to death. In spite of his unenviable circumstances, though, Paul mustered the strength and courage to stand trial in his own defense and tell his story to a Roman governor named Felix.

Felix was a guy living far from God, but Acts 24:26–27 records that for two years following that occasion, Paul met privately with him to discuss spiritual matters. Two years Paul invested in this man, and there is no indication in Scripture that Felix *ever* came to faith in Christ. But is there any wiser investment to make? I guarantee that Paul never resented, even for a moment, the time he devoted to Felix's journey. I'd be as shocked as you to hear Paul count even *one* of those moments as wasted!

And like Paul, all Christ-followers who "get" what it means to be used by the Holy Spirit are thrilled with any opportunity to help move a person even an eighth of a millimeter closer to God. True joy in the Christian adventure unfurls when you play the role that the Spirit asks you to play. Your job — and mine — is to say, "God, I am open for whatever role you might have me play. Whatever it is, I'm available to be used."

THE OTHER SIDE OF SEED-SOWING

It's true that walk-across-the-room people experience the best this life has to offer. But if you're anything like me, you'll have to fight tooth-and-nail to stay in the game. Because although the home runs have been invigorating, my batting average over the years is abysmally low.

For each touching illustration I offer about walking across a room and witnessing something miraculous unfold, I could recount several hundred occasions when walks across rooms never left even a wrinkle. Times when I invested in people—loved, served, and cared for them; shared the gospel with them; put my heart on a platter on their behalf—and absolutely nothing productive happened.

Nothing I could detect this side of heaven, anyway.

At Willow Creek, we refer to the lobby benches just outside of the auditorium as the "Fools' Bench." Every weekend, at least a handful of Willow members sit out there waiting for people to show up. They can be anyone—a boss, a friend, a family member, you name it. But in every case, they've prayed for these people and taken walks across rooms for these people, hoping beyond hope to have a little spiritual impact in their lives.

So someone in our congregation finally musters the courage to invite his friend to church and is stunned when the person says yes. *They're actually going to come!* the Willow person thinks. Sunday finally comes and he stands out there in the lobby, anxiously awaiting his friend's arrival. A few minutes pass, and the pacing begins. Back and forth. Back and forth. The futile pacing leads to fervent praying. "Oh, God, please prompt this person to show up. Come on, God!" Fifteen minutes elapse, and he realizes that no one is coming. But he can't bring himself to give up just yet. So he decides to have a seat—just wait five more minutes, maybe. On a lobby bench. On the Fools' Bench, waiting for someone who agreed to come but who is clearly not going to show up.

He looks over and sees another Willow person pacing. "So who are you waiting for?" he ventures. "Well, my boss," she sighs. "I've worked on him for six years. And finally, this weekend, he said he'd come."

Ah, just another fool like me, the Willow guy thinks.

·　·　·　·　•

I stood in the bullpen after a weekend service one time and was approached by a young man who was sobbing uncontrollably. He finally formed a few sentences and conveyed that he'd only asked for one thing for his birthday—that his dad would come to church with him. His dad had agreed to come, so the kid sat out there on the lobby benches for the entire service.

You can guess the rest of the story, and this kid's lament said it all: "Man, this is hard."

You know what? It *is* hard. Maybe this is why Paul encourages doing the "work" of evangelism. It is work, and hard work at that. You put your heart out there. You offer grace and acceptance and love to people far from God. You sow seed. You make the phone calls. You extend the hand of friendship. You pick up the phone in the middle of the night. And at the end of the day, you just feel like you've been ripped to shreds. But somehow you hang in there, determined to keep sowing seed. Sure, you may be a fool, but you're a special kind of fool. You're the fool who still believes that a tiny green sprout will one day rise up from the dirt.

·   ·   ·   ·   •

A few months ago, some of my senior staff and I met in the private room of a restaurant for a day-long brainstorming meeting. At the lunch hour, three men walked into the main dining room where our team was just sitting down for lunch. They noticed me and made a beeline for our table, customary mischief written all over their faces.

After greeting me warmly, they asked if the rest of the group worked with me at the church. My colleagues all nodded as a few of them introduced themselves to the threesome.

"Well, you need to find yourselves a new pastor to work for!" they howled. "Because this guy has tried to straighten us out for over twenty-five years and has failed with all three of us!"

One of them then reminisced about late-night conversations we'd had that never really went anywhere. Another talked about how many books and tapes he had received from me: instead of reading or listening to them, he explained with a grin, he chose to "recycle" them.

The stories flowed freely, the mood in the room very lighthearted and jovial. Obviously, they felt comfortable enough with me to have some laughs at my expense in front of my team.

After they excused themselves and went to go find the hostess, I looked each staff member in the eye and said, "They were telling the absolute truth. I don't think I've made a single dent in any of their lives in twenty-five years. I've tried. I've prayed. I've loved them. Listened to them and served them at various points in their lives, but from where I sit, it's all just been a bust. But regardless of that reality, I am going to keep sowing seed for all I'm worth, praying for the day that the soil will soften a bit."

That being said, though, they might be right about needing to find a better leader!

WHEN FOOLS GET THEIR DUE

In my neighborhood, Tuesday nights are Garbage Night. I know this because in our house, I'm Garbage Guy. So every Tuesday night, I wheel the garbage container down the driveway and get everything all set for the Wednesday morning pickup.

Several years ago a gentleman and his family moved to our neighborhood into a house with a driveway just a few yards from ours. Every Tuesday night, he would bring his garbage out. It was ironic how week after week, he and I would wheel out our garbage cans at precisely the same time. Nine o'clock would roll around, and sure enough, we would see each other heading down the driveway.

On one particular Tuesday night, I remember seeing him from a distance and feeling prompted by the Holy Spirit to walk across the cul-de-sac. I caught my breath and agreed with the Spirit that I should approach him, even if to introduce myself and be done with it. "Here we go," I nervously mumbled to myself. "Let's see what happens with this one."

So I walked across the road, stuck out my hand, and said, "Hey, you just moved in, right? My name is Bill." He took my hand, smiled, and said, "Well, this ought to be easy. My name's Bill too."

Instantly, we hit it off. And from that point forward, almost every Tuesday night presented a fresh opportunity to engage in conversation, find out about each other's families and interests, and begin to build a friendship. A few weeks into this dynamic, he finally asked me what I did for a living. "Well, I'm the pastor of a church in the area—"

Before I could finish my sentence, he said, "Not the one that ties up traffic all over!"

"Uh, probably not that one," I lied.

"Well, Bill," he said with a big grin, "this ought to be easy too. I don't go to church!"

I agreed he'd sort of summed things up on that front and switched gears to what he did for a living.

"I own a Chevrolet dealership about forty-five minutes from here," he said.

"Wouldn't you know! This is easy all the way around," I said. "I would *never* buy a Chevrolet!"

Our back-and-forth Tuesday night bantering went on this way for quite some time, always while standing around a few garbage cans. I knew how he felt about church, but after enough time had elapsed, I felt an open door to invite him to Willow. One morning when Easter was approaching, assuming Bill had no plans to darken a church's doorstep for Sunday services, I said, "You know, Bill, you're a lousy citizen—how can you even claim to be a good red-blooded American—especially a Republican!—unless you go to church on *Easter*! I mean, what's the matter with you?" (He had it coming ... and it worked.)

Annoyed that I had challenged his patriotism, he agreed to come to Willow's Easter service that Sunday. The following Tuesday night, around nine o'clock as always, he and I brought our garbage out to the curb. He started talking even before he reached me. "Church has *changed*! I mean, people were normal; the service was great. It was absolutely amazing at Willow Creek, Bill. And do you want to hear the most surprising thing of all?"

I began rattling off in my mind all the things he could be referring to. The size of the building. The energy of the crowds during Easter weekend. The incredible singing or drama or stage set.

He interrupted my train of thought: "It just never occurred to me that you could *talk* in front of people!"

I checked my ego at my garbage can and reminded myself that for a lot of folks, the jury was still out on that one. He said, "You know, we chat at the garbage cans and all that, but I never dreamed that you could talk in front of real people. I loved your Easter message, Bill. I just loved it!"

Many months passed—I didn't want to badger the man, after all—but on a garbage-can trip one evening, I said, "Hey Bill, just one small thing. Six months ago, you said that you really enjoyed coming to church at Easter and that you just *loved* my talk. And then you never came back. Can you help me out here?"

He didn't even flinch. "Your sermon was *so* good," he said, "that it has lasted me all this time!" His comment, mixed with the too-big grin on his face, told me that this was probably why Bill was such a good car salesman.

All I know is that God must have had a good chuckle when he elected to make us neighbors.

As time went on, Bill and his family doubled their attendance. Now they made their way to Willow every Easter *and* Christmas, just like clockwork. After the first cycle of his Easter/Christmas routine, he said, "I don't know what's come over me! I've been to church *twice* this year. This is unbe*lie*vable!" Must have gone on for five or six years this way, and each time he nearly broke his arm patting himself on the back for his commendable record.

·   ·   ·   ·   •

On a Tuesday night following the Christmas break one year, we both wheeled our cans down the driveways, fending off the icy Chicago wind. We chatted for a few moments before I made leave-taking motions, explaining that it was way too cold to be outside.

As I turned to head back to the house, he said, "Hey, by the way, you know that Christmas Eve service? Well, I accepted Christ there." *You what?* I thought as he kept talking. "I asked Christ to come into my life—I really did. And I want him to have the top spot in my world."

No kidding, I thought. Instantaneously, my desire to escape the freezing cold was replaced with a desire to freeze that moment in time. If I could have stopped the planet from spinning—just for a split second—to savor Bill's acceptance of Christ, I would have.

Friends, I've said it before, and I'll say it again: that experience is enough for me.

I don't need much more in life than a series of those moments, when people far from God begin responding to his gentle nudging and then see their eternities changed. I was practically levitating the entire night.

Bill gave me a probing look and said, "Listen, I don't know what all of this means, and I'm probably not going to go through some dramatic, overnight transformation, but I know that that's what I want. I want to move in the direction of putting Christ at the top, if you'll help me."

· · · · •

After that night, what had been innocuous dialogue at those garbage cans became a full-fledged course in Christianity 101. We talked about the progress he was making in his spiritual life and about books I'd given him to read—that he actually read.

Lately, we have been making progress in understanding the fundamental core of Christianity, which is simply a relationship with God. We talk about becoming more aware of God's companionship throughout the course of his day, remembering that not only does God love us, but he actually likes us too. We talk about how he will sense God's smile on his life as he seeks to become obedient to him. We discuss these things called "promptings" and how to listen to the Spirit's nudging. And how, over time, he will learn to be used by God as he responds to the whispers of God's Spirit.

Several months ago, he said something incredible: "You know, Bill, if there are people over at Willow who are struggling financially, maybe some single moms or people whose businesses have collapsed, I'm a car guy, and I might be able to help."

Bill had received a prompting several days earlier to explore the possibility of providing two cars to Willow families in need. "In the middle of my workday this week," he said, "I suddenly realized that I had two cars at the dealership available if anyone needs them." His next question brought a smile to my face: "Would that be something you think I should do?"

"Yeah," I said. "If that's something God is laying on your heart to do, then it would be a good idea to go ahead and do it." So Bill and a couple of men drove the cars right to the front of the church on a weekday afternoon, and I watched them hand over the keys to my brother Dan, who led the CARS ministry—Christian Auto Repairmen Serving, a group devoted to fixing up donated cars from our congregation and repositioning them into the lives of single-parent families at Willow.

That day, I caught a glimpse of an overjoyed version of my once-materialistic neighbor. By his own admission, he had lived for money; and yet here he was, taking his hard-won earnings and giving them joyfully for the sake of the adventure of following Christ.

The next Tuesday night, Bill told me that bringing those cars to the church was one of the most significant moments of his entire life. Giving a couple of cars to a few people in need changed one man's life forever.

As I recount that story, I'm reminded of the reason we keep on sowing seed. Because once in a blue moon, we have that magical experience of being present with someone when the fertile soil of their heart and the strategic placement of the seed we sow collide. Not because of some well-orchestrated plan or some well-intentioned formula. Just because we have been faithful to listen to the Holy Spirit and play the role we're intended to play.

It's true—the moment you feel as though your evangelistic effectiveness has bottomed out is the exact moment when God intervenes with graciousness. As you prove faithful to sow seed, even with skepticism about whether they will ever germinate, you will suddenly see rich black soil appear. For me, there is no greater reward this side of heaven!

STUDY QUESTIONS

1. What evangelistic "fads" have you seen emerge throughout the course of your life? Did you participate in any of them? If so, what was your experience like?

2. Galatians 5:25 says that "since we live by the Spirit, let us keep in step with the Spirit." What would change about your perception of evangelism if your number one priority was to "keep in step with the Spirit" rather than memorizing formulas or winning souls?

3. Have you ever experienced what you would call "Spirit-directed promptings?" If so, describe a time when you knew God was asking you to do or say something. Did you obey the prompting? What was the experience like?

4. Take another look at the story of the staff member who wanted me to meet with a community leader on pages 43–45. How do you think I knew that I should go through with the meeting? In your own life, how do you know when to follow a prompting and when to stick to your day's agenda as scheduled?

5. Throughout Scripture, God conveys his desire to communicate with his children. Consider the sentiment expressed below, quoted from page 37. Why is this type of attitude so critical in the life of a Christ-follower?

   These days, I try to wake up each morning declaring, "My life is in *your* hands, God. Use me to point someone toward you today—I promise to cooperate in any way I can. If you want me to say a word for you today, I'll do that. If you want me to keep quiet but demonstrate love and servanthood, by your Spirit's power I will. I'm *fully* available to you today, so guide me by your Spirit."

6. Do you really believe that someday the seed you sow will fall on the right soil and produce fruit? Why or why not? How would taking Christ at his word that you *will* produce fruit encourage you to get engaged in the work of evangelism?

PART II

Living in 3D

CHAPTER 3

First, Develop Friendships

. . . . .

Recently, the management team at Willow convened for an all-day session in downtown Chicago to map out plans for a new neighborhood evangelism strategy. Our suburban neighborhoods are seeing hundreds of new rooftops appear, and we realized we needed to better equip our members for introducing a God-ward element into their relationships with people who live down the street, around the corner, or right next door. The goal was simple: come up with a way to enfold friends and neighbors in Chicagoland with the love of Christ—and do so *naturally.*

Our executive pastor stood at a flip chart, fat marker in hand, prompting us to distill our thoughts to the fundamental idea—the nut—of what we were really talking about. A few minutes into our discussion, one of my colleagues had a revelation unfold. "Isn't this … isn't the whole *thing* about seeing how many neighbors we can take to heaven with us? Can't we boil it down to looking at people who live within a bike ride of our houses, seeing how many of them we can take to heaven with us through the work of Christ?"

Everyone looked around the room as heads started to bob and energy began to rise. "Yeah. It doesn't have to be more complicated than that, does it?"

Think of it: when you got up today, whether you walked into an office complex, a construction site, an office, a classroom, the local grocery store, you were probably surrounded by a sea of faces—some belonging to friends you know and family members you treasure, others belonging to perfect strangers. Just imagine the shift in your focus if you made a habit of approaching *all* of them with this attitude: *My ultimate goal is to see how many of these people I can have on each elbow when I cross the finish line of this earthly life and run into God's presence for all of eternity!*

We immediately assigned one of our senior staff members, Garry Poole, to the role of testing out ways to achieve this goal in a few nearby neighborhoods. Soon Garry identified three distinct concepts that must be present to have maximum impact in our communities. Eventually, we coined the entire approach "Living in 3D." When effective walk-across-the-room people interact with others in their world, they

Develop friendships—by engaging in the lives of people around them

Discover stories—before sharing their own story and God's redemptive story

Discern next steps—by following the Holy Spirit's direction

Most Christ-followers agree with these ideas. If you ask a hundred believers whether they have friends or family members who are living far from God and who face a Christless eternity, they will all say yes.

And if you ask the same group if they agree that our goal is to walk into heaven with as many of those people as possible by building relationships, understanding where they are in their faith journeys, and seizing opportunities to tell the story of God's love for them, again, most will agree.

But sit that group of a hundred down, look them directly in the eyes, and ask whether they are actively *doing the work* of telling their lost friends and family members about how to have a relationship with God. What do you think they'll say? It's conjecture, but based on my experience, you'll be lucky to find half of them engaged in the process. In short, Christ-followers don't disagree with the need for people to be pointed toward God. They just struggle with how to get it done.

So before we dive into the nuances of how to "live in 3D," let me first address *who* is responsible for the work of evangelism.

THE LIFE CYCLE OF MOST CHRIST-FOLLOWERS

On average, 30 percent of the people who approach me after weekend services at Willow have one thing on their minds: how to get one of their lost friends or family members found. Whether it's a dad or an uncle or a neighbor or a boss who is spiritually adrift, countless numbers of Christ-followers throughout the course of a ministry year express their heartfelt concern for someone far from God.

Each time, I offer the same question in response to these good-hearted men and women. And each time, my suggestion is met with their disbelief. "Why don't *you* help point them to God?" I ask. Almost to a person, the idea itself seems ludicrous: *I could never do that! I just wouldn't know what to say. That's really not my gift. Not my personality. I would screw it up. And anyway, that's what you [professionals] are for!*

Not surprisingly, the Bible puts a different spin on things. Simply put, if you are a Christ-follower, then you are called, equipped, and expected to share the gospel. No exceptions! Leighton Ford, former vice president of the Billy Graham Evangelistic Association, summed it up this way: "A church which bottlenecks its specialists to do its witnessing is living in violation of both [Jesus Christ] and the consistent pattern of the early Christians. Evangelism was the task of the *whole church*, not just the 'name characters'" (emphasis mine).

Somehow, though, despite the noble desire to get lost people found, many have abdicated their role in the process altogether. As I have traveled around the world visiting pastors and volunteer leaders, I've developed a deep concern for a dangerous trend that is alive and well in many evangelical churches. The longer a person attends church, the fewer evangelistic discussions they engage in with family members and friends. Fewer presentations of the life-changing plan of salvation are given, and fewer invitations to events that attractively present the message of Christ are offered, mostly because Christ-followers have fewer friends outside the faith to whom to offer them.

In the graph, the horizontal axis represents how long you have walked with Christ,

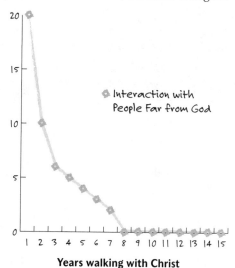

Interaction with People Far from God

Years walking with Christ

noted in one-year increments. The vertical axis represent the amount of quality contact you have had with people who are living far from God. Statistics—as well as my own empirical observations—reflect that shortly after a Christ-follower makes a faith decision, contact with people outside the Christian faith actually decreases. Business meetings are used solely for tackling the task at hand instead of being leveraged for cracking open previously dead-bolted doors, spiritually speaking. Family functions are seen as platforms to take relational backbiting to a new level instead of being treated as opportunities to make some spiritual headway. Errands are run with one eye on the clock and the other on the to-do list, with zero consideration given to the needs of the clerk standing at the checkout or the person refilling the prescription.

This trend spirals downward year after year until Christ-followers face their dying day and realize they have become completely insulated in an evangelism-void vacuum. They lament the fact that at the hour just before they meet God face-to-face, they are at their all-time evangelistic low. And here's what sobers my heart: rather than an isolated case or two, I believe that this is the path of *nearly every* average Christian.

Right now some of you are thinking, *You know, Bill, I understand the point you're making, but not everyone's good at the evangelism thing.*

Perhaps you're the type who agrees that evangelism needs to happen. You really do *want* for people to be directed toward God. But somewhere along the way, you decided that the task is reserved for spiritual superstars who can muscle a faith discussion into any conversation, anywhere, anytime. Your self-talk goes something like this: "I don't have the right confidence level or the right skills. I don't have the quick mind, the relational aptitude, or the gift mix. I just don't have what it takes." Some of you really do believe, for one reason or another, that you are disqualified from or ill-equipped for the work of evangelism.

For those of you in this category, what perplexes me about your paradigm is the disequilibrium that must characterize your life. Here's my point: If you genuinely think that evangelism should be a critical function in the life of a Christ-follower, but you also fully believe that you are unfit to evangelize, at some point don't you have to reconcile the two? I'm just curious how you live inside of that reality without the pressure to share your faith weighing you down and without guilt utterly overtaking you.

HORSE-TRADING WITH GOD

The issue used to really stump me, but over the years I've seen something play out that begins to address how many people salve their consciences: they make horse trades with God—little side bargains with the King of the universe. Sure, they'd never admit this in front of civilized people, but privately they come to God and say, "I'm really not cut out to take walks across rooms, God. I'm terribly uncomfortable with risk, edge, and adventure. And frankly, this whole 'mystical' realm is more unnerving than I can even articulate!"

They continue to chatter away to God, secretly hoping he'll momentarily withhold his response while they hurriedly get to the best part of the arrangement. "But here's my deal, God. I will get all over spiritual development. I will be a Bible knowledge hound! If you want, I'll throw myself into building Habitat for Humanity homes—every summer, in fact. I will climb all over volunteerism—I'll show up at church five nights a week if you ask me to. You let me off the evangelism hook, and I'll prove my love for you in half a dozen other ways if it kills me. That's my deal."

Friends, I've watched these horse-trades happen all over the kingdom, in churches large and small. Just little evangelism exchanges—seemingly innocent deals that if struck are really win-win, wouldn't you say? I mean, the Christ-follower gets off the hook, and God gets freed up to go chase down someone who has a stronger evangelism gift.

My blood pressure rises just writing about it.

·   ·   ·   ·   •

If Christ-followers' tactics only went this far, I would still hang my head in dismay at the selfishness and ugliness of it all. But things can get even worse than this. I've seen scores of Christ-followers get so cut off, having horse-traded away any sense of responsibility or adventure about reaching people, that they actually get *annoyed* with those outside of the kingdom of God.

Instead of walking toward people who need God's redemptive love, they step into a mode of no longer wanting anything to do with them. Self-proclaimed followers of Jesus Christ develop an aversion to nonbelievers, going to all lengths to avoid the exact people Christ came to redeem.

Again, no one in a right mind would own up to this out loud, but I watch it go on below the surface—in a person's mind and heart—all the time. A Christ-follower says, "I'm so sick and tired of the filthy mouth of this guy at work. I can't stand his language! I hate his jokes and how he lives." Or "You wouldn't believe the morals of my neighbor, the partying she does. And my boss? You should see his voting patterns. If I could vote *him* outta here, I would!"

The aversion can become so intense that a Christ-follower has to plumb new depths of dysfunction to deal with it. "Here's what I think I'll do," she says. "I'll set my alarm so that in the morning, I'll get up to Christian music. I'll email my Christian girlfriends all throughout the course of my workday so that I can stay pumped up with Christian thoughts. At break time, coffee time, lunchtime, I'm going to sit by myself and read my Bible.

"Then I will fill up my evenings with family and church activities, and (if I watch television at all) it's only Christian shows for me. I'll go to bed, wake up tomorrow, and start all over with Step One. My life will stay exactly how I want it to be: simple and safe. Spotless and uncluttered. Protected and predictable. Just the way I like it."

And if I'm forced to nail it down, I see only one problem with this cocooning pattern: it is the polar opposite of the way of Christ. Simple and safe was not exactly the theme Christ was championing when he warned his followers that being sent out as lambs among wolves was part of the deal. "Spotless and uncluttered" had no place in the task of embracing a dying, broken, weary world with radical forgiveness and actionable love.

THE LIFE CYCLE CHRIST ENCOURAGES

I believe that once you really grasp the mission God has asked you to participate in while you're sucking air here on planet earth, you just can't help but to spill out the love you've been given. In his book entitled *Christianity 101*, Dr. Gilbert Bilezikian says that "God is perfectly self-sufficient within the grandeur of his transcendence. He did not create humans in order to give himself companionship. Quite the opposite: He gave life out of love."[3] Friends, true love can't be contained—it must spill over.

This is where living in 3D always begins—with love. The Bible teaches that as you see patterns move up and to the right in things like walking with God, maturing in your faith, and growing in Christlikeness, then—as the chart below depicts—you should see a corresponding *increase* in your love for people and in your propensity to reach out to them in friendship.

Devoted followers of Christ acknowledge that what God treasures *first* (and there is no close second) is people. They open themselves up to the promptings of God's Spirit, putting one foot in front of the other as they reach out to lonely or disillusioned or sin-scarred folks, living out with abandon what it means to be the ones who walk across rooms. As they continue to walk closely with God, they receive added insight about who

God is and begin to experience the pattern of God's faithfulness in their lives. They receive more answers to prayer; see more manifestations of God's grace; grow in understanding of God's heart for people; and become increasingly more intentional regarding evangelism.

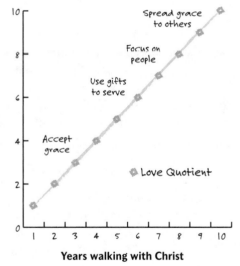

Have you noticed this in your own life? The longer you walk with God, the more open your arms become. Instead of clenching tightly to a small circle of insiders, you throw out your arms, opening them up to those outside the circle who may need to come in. As your arms grow wider in worship, they correspondingly grow wider in acceptance.

The idea is this: by the end of your life, your heart is so tender, your vision so clear, that you grab doctors, nurses, lost family members, the hospital janitor, anyone, and tell them, "God loves you! I'm about to head out of here, but please know that he loves you." And then—boom—you die. But just before you do, this thought strikes you: *I was doing the very*

*best thing I could possibly be doing, offering the best gift I could possibly offer
just before I took flight.*

·   ·   ·   ·   •

Several months before The Passion of the Christ *opened in movie theaters,* I
had the privilege of seeing a preview of the film. Near the end, I sat there
awestruck as I soaked up the powerful moments just before Jesus died on
the cross. He had just endured one of many beatings and was found suffering through a horrendous crucifixion. As he started to inhale his last
breath, a rogue criminal hanging on an adjacent cross made a plea. "You
know, if a guy like me could wind up in the kingdom you're headed to,
that would just be amazing." (This from a man who had *royally* screwed
up, as far as we know. People didn't normally get capital punishment for
jaywalking.)

Jesus' response to this career criminal is absolutely fascinating to me.
Without an ounce of deliberation, he gave grace to the guy. "Today you
will be with me in my kingdom," he told the repentant.

Friends, *that* is the model. The same propensity to give grace in all
situations ought to be true of your life and of mine. If we share the dream
to become radically loving, outwardly focused, grace-giving people, then
we ought to be the first ones to expand our hearts and invite folks to come
into the kingdom.

I wonder if this is how you approach everyone you meet. I wonder if
this is your posture as you seek to develop friendships that may one day
lead to a person getting enfolded by God's grace. Try a little experiment
with me this week. As you pull into your driveway, fight the temptation
to look past your neighbor. Perhaps for the first time, stop long enough to
wonder why God chose to put the two of you on the same block to begin
with. When you drop off your dry cleaning, take four seconds to smile,
and ask the name of the person standing behind the counter. If he or she
has served you well, then say so. When you run into the drugstore to pick
up your prescription, take a good look at the clerk who's assisting you.
What's that person's story? Will you carve out two minutes to find out?
Or should you bump into your mail carrier during the day, invest a few
moments in discovering if he or she has a spouse or kids—what do they
like to do around town when it's a day off?

You can do this type of thing. You can become someone who gives grace away so freely that when people far from God think of *you*, they immediately think of "grace" next. "What do I think of Tom? Well, the first thing that comes to mind is that he's full of grace. I could honestly say that if I messed up in a big way, he's a guy I'd call. If I landed on his doorstep after a huge mistake or tragedy, I could count on him giving me compassion instead of judgment and understanding rather than a tongue-lashing."

I would *love* for that to be said of me! In fact, I'd love for it to be said of all Christ-followers.

SPOTTING POTENTIAL

Better than anyone in history, in any field or discipline, Jesus capitalized on the possibility in people — the *hidden potential* inherent in all of us. Talented entrepreneurs in our society see hidden potential in a product or service before anybody else does — and as a result of pursuing their vision, cutting-edge companies emerge. Expert athletic coaches often spot hidden potential in a high school football player or tennis player, and because of applied foresight, college sports dynasties are built.

But Jesus had a corner on the "potential" market. He had an uncanny ability to look past the obvious flaws in people's lives and envision who they could become if the power of God were released in their lives. Intrinsically, he just *wondered* about people. Wondered what they could become. Wondered how they might look in a transformed state. Wondered what impact they could have if their lives were invested in things of eternal value.

He somehow saw the godly worshiper clothed as a worn, wearied prostitute. The faithful disciple hiding inside a fisherman named Simon. The hidden philanthropist in the life of a crooked tax collector named Zacchaeus. The risk-taker in a cowardly Jewish ruler named Nicodemus. What a fantastic gift he had for seeing what nobody else could see!

"All things are possible" was Jesus' mantra. *All* things. And countless lives were transformed because he chose to look past surface stuff to see what was ultimately possible.

Acts 9 records the dramatic transformation of Saul the murderer becoming Paul the apostle. Most likely in his early thirties and undoubtedly one of the most promising, zealous young Jews around, Saul seemed to have the world by the tail.

One day, he and a group of traveling companions were headed to a town called Damascus, bound and determined to wipe out the remaining members of "the Way." As far as he knew, Jesus had already been killed. So the only thing left to do was to capture the last few Christ-followers and bring them to trial.

The group rode along minding their own business when suddenly a blinding light from heaven appeared and knocked Saul off his donkey. Understandably, his buddies were rendered speechless. As Saul, literally blinded by the experience, leaned in closer, he sensed Jesus Christ in the brilliant blaze.

"Saul, why do you persecute me?" he heard Jesus ask.

And utterly awestruck after encountering the resurrected Lord, Saul the persecutor became Paul the apostle. Kingdom dissident became kingdom-builder. Antagonist was now ally. Foe became *friend*.

I'm sure that the Christians in Damascus who were nervously awaiting Saul's arrival couldn't believe their ears when they heard the news of Saul's conversion. "Saul?! Redeemed? *Surely* not. I mean, how does a hard guy like Saul suddenly get softened?"

Obviously, Jesus knew the answer.

Jesus' supernatural vision regarding people's potential gave him irrepressible optimism as he engaged with vagrants, liars, cowards, and crooks. To them all, the promise was the same. The old *can* become new, Jesus said. The fallen *can* be restored. The prideful *can* be humbled. The wanderers *can* come home. The weak *can* become strong. Derelicts *can* become disciples. At its core, this is what it means to develop friendships with spiritual goals in mind.

Jesus truly believed in the power of God to transform human lives—a belief that motivated his insatiable pursuit of all sorts of people at all points on the spiritual spectrum. He was fierce in his determination to look past ill-timed comments and inappropriate actions. He dreamed about what could happen in a person's life if God's power were released in them—and so he pushed through people's fear and sin, and he kept including people, loving people, and lifting people up to their fullest potential.

∘   ∘   ∘   ∘   •

At Willow Creek, we've historically placed a high value on church involvement through what we call a "Participating Member process." As people become active in our church for the first time, it is a means through which they come to understand their identity in Christ, their role in the church, and the expectations God places on them in areas such as spiritual development, financial stewardship, and community life.

Every month, as part of this process, we celebrate the arrival of new members by having them share their testimonies just before our midweek New Community service. Recently, I had the opportunity to sit in one of our auditorium seats and soak up their stories.

One small-group leader stood in front of the thousands of people gathered there and said, "It was a *big* deal when I became a participating member of this church two years ago. But tonight, I am here to celebrate the fact that two couples from our small group are becoming members. And it's funny — I'm actually more excited about these folks' membership than my own. Maybe because I believe God used me in some small way to help them find their way."

Why is it so easy to forget that wrapping caring arms around another person gives back far more than it takes?

I stood in the back with tears in my eyes, remembering what I had learned years before — that there is unparalleled joy in knowing that God is using *you* to shape and mold another person's life.

As you view people through this lens — what I call "radical inclusiveness" — you have new eyes to see things as Jesus saw them. You allow people's foibles and failings and faults to fall away, instead seeing them in their potential, Spirit-infused state. You see filthy-mouthed, party-loving, woman-chasing Joe, and you say, "What would Joe — even a guy like Joe — be like if God ruled and reigned in his heart? Joe would be incredible if Christ invaded his world!"

You start dreaming of that day, in fact. You begin picturing him in his redeemed state. Your love for him grows and grows as you move toward him, engaging in the good, the bad, and the ugly of his life. You find yourself craving opportunities to be around people just like him — people who are one prayer away from becoming your eternal brothers and sisters.

CAN YOU SEE IT?

Over the Christmas break one year, my family and I accepted an invitation to a holiday party while on vacation. A friend who would be attending the same party tipped me off about an older businessman who had been vacationing in the same community for years. "I'm sure he'll be at the party," this friend began. "Look, just be aware that he's been through a divorce, and he's living with a woman now who's not his wife. He's into drinking … a lot of drinking. And … well, he *knows* who you are. He won't be too thrilled to bump into you at a party, you know, in a social setting like this. I wanted you to be forewarned, that's all."

I walked away from that conversation thinking, *Give me a real challenge!* Or more the case, *Give God a real challenge!* I'd seen my fair share of crass, brazen men become tenderhearted once the Holy Spirit supernaturally intervened. I had stood there utterly amazed on many occasions as former druggies and adulterers and atheists softened to discussions of a spiritual nature. And each time, my belief was renewed that the Holy Spirit can accomplish outright miracles when Christ-followers stick their necks out in conveying the hope of the gospel.

That evening, my family and I arrived at the host couple's home as planned. As I headed into the living room, I careened into a gentleman who fit the general description of the businessman my friend had warned me about. Recovering, I stuck out my hand and said, "Hi, my name's Bill." He recognized who I was and sort of grunted as if to say, "Yeah, yeah, save it, buddy."

"We're kind of starting cold here, aren't we?" I laughed. He told me his name, and I immediately realized that this was in fact the guy I was supposed to avoid offending that evening. *He* would *be the first person I run into,* I thought.

Fumbling for some reasonable way to redeem our bumpy start, I asked him how long he'd been vacationing there and why he had chosen this particular spot over other places. Somewhere in his response, he mentioned that he loved the warmer climates … and that he had been a boater for nearly four decades.

"What a coincidence! I love boating!" I blurted out. I cautioned him that if we started down the boat path, he'd never get me to shut up.

"Do you have a boat?" he said, as if shocked to discover that I was human. I began explaining the whole thing, the words tumbling out of my mouth—how I had fallen headlong into a love affair with boating and sailboat racing, what kinds of boats I'd sailed, my favorite waters, the fact that my son, only twenty-three at the time, had recently sailed solo from South Haven, Michigan, all through the Great Lakes, out the New York barge canal, all the way down to Florida, and eventually throughout most of the Bahamas island chain. "Here! Meet my son, Todd!" I said as I prodded Todd toward the man.

"You're *both* boaters!" he exclaimed. "How about that!" As we continued chatting, I could tell his preconceived ideas about me were dissipating into thin air. By this time, he was anxious to keep talking—to me an indication of the open door I'd hoped for.

"So how did you get down here?" he asked.

I explained that my family had flown down commercially this time, which somehow led to him telling me all about the private plane that he always brought to this particular location. Stunned, I said, "You have a plane? How about that! I got my pilot's license when I was sixteen."

"Me too!" he laughed. "What are the chances? Same age and everything. What kind of ratings do you have?"

We talked planes for the next twenty minutes, and once that conversation exhausted itself, we started down the what-you-do-for-a-living path. It turned out that the one and only person I knew who worked in the same industry as this man was a good friend of his. "I can't believe you know him!" he nearly shouted. And silently I thought, *Of course I know him. How typical of God!*

Of *course* God put this man right by the door as I entered the party. Of *course* God saw to it that there were common denominators for us to discover. Of *course* God gave me a few hints about what to say, how to respond, and how to listen well. Of *course* God allowed for a bridge to be built there, instead of deepening the cliché chasm that says the "God guy" and the "pagan guy" just can't relate.

After we got over the initial shock of sharing a mutual acquaintance, I said, "Well, here's one you'll enjoy. Less than a week ago, your good friend came to a party in my home after attending a Christmas Eve service at our church."

The guy's voice was drenched with disbelief. "He *never* goes to church," he said. "I *know* he never goes to church."

"Well, he came to church and actually said he loved it," I said, which elicited a "No *way!*" from the businessman. We had a good laugh and then went our separate ways to mingle with others at the party, continuing the conversation periodically throughout the night. Each time I'd spot him from across the room, I'd have a good chuckle with God. *I can just see it, God,* I'd think. *I can see exactly what this guy will be like once you rock his world!*

At the end of the evening in a clandestine gesture, he slid a business card in my hand. "The next time you're in Chicago and I'm in Chicago," he said, "I might buy you dinner. And who knows, you may be able to drag me to that church of yours."

·   ·   ·   ·   •

As he walked out the door that night, I thought about all of the dynamics at work in how that whole deal unfolded. He had been forewarned that I would be there, and in his mind I had a huge target on my forehead from the moment I entered the house. If I had played my "God card" immediately —telling him how I loved being a Christian and how he should become one too—things would have headed south in a heartbeat.

Instead, I just focused on building rapport with him, telling him about things that I truly enjoy in addition to God. I have lots of meaningful pursuits in life that center on God and his redemptive kingdom agenda. But I also have passionate interest in other things, two of which are boating and flying. And I feel enormous freedom to talk about interests I love, both regarding God and regarding things other than God.

I hope that as you engage in the world around you, you'll go for broke in your interactions with people, starting with the ones right in front of you. Be the one who catches the vision for how the man or woman standing in front of you will look once God's redeeming power does its work in his or her life.

SERVING A WITHERED WORLD

At one point during Jesus' earthly ministry, the Pharisees had grown so tired of him correcting, silencing, and disregarding them that they birthed a plot to have Jesus caught breaking their beloved Law. According to

Mark 3, Jesus was teaching in the synagogue one day while a man with a deformed hand was sitting there. The Pharisees got excited once they noticed that Jesus was going nuts trying to teach the Scriptures while a sick person helplessly sat ten feet from him. Surely he'd stop his talk and heal the guy! And on the Sabbath, no less—what a controversy this would cause! *This is going to be perfect!* the Pharisees thought as they watched with bated breath.

Pure speculation at this point, but can't you imagine the scene? A handful of Pharisees are seen traipsing about town to hunt down some poor, unsuspecting person. Suddenly, they spot their man: a guy is sitting there on a bench, his withered hand in plain sight.

The Pharisees spring into action. "This is your lucky day, sir! Come with us! Right this way; we have a front-row seat reserved for you in the synagogue, and Jesus is up today ... what are the *chances*?" They bring this man in and sit him down, and Jesus takes center stage to begin teaching. As he surveys his audience, he notices this man with a withered hand. He glances over at the religious leaders, noticing that they are all poised on the edge of their seats, wondering if the snare they had set that day was going to do the trick.

Jesus sizes up the whole twisted situation. Mark 3:5 says that he looked around at them with anger, deeply distressed at their stubborn hearts. Here were these "leaders"—men who were known as the religious elite—behaving mercilessly as they completely disregarded a broken man's misery.

Jesus knew that the Pharisees permitted healing on the Sabbath in life-threatening cases but that this man's condition was not life-threatening. He knew that the Pharisees couldn't care less about this crippled man or his family or his future or his eternity. He also knew what was at stake should he choose to heal him.

Without any hesitation, Jesus suddenly speaks to the man with the withered hand. "Stand up!" he says. "Stretch out your hand and come forward."

The man does a double-take. *Me? Really? You're really going to heal me?* Jesus heals the man on the spot, thereby sealing his own fate with the Pharisees, who notify the Herodians of Jesus' indiscretion—the same people who eventually have Jesus arrested and killed.

*   *   *   *   *

The story of the withered-hand man ends there in Scripture, but don't you wonder what it was like in those quiet moments after everyone had fled the synagogue and only Jesus and the good-as-new man stood there? In my imagination, I picture the guy looking at Jesus, his Great Healer, and saying, "Uh, did I get you into trouble or anything? I mean, it seems like there was some tension in the room just then."

And I envision Jesus saying, "Nah, don't worry about it. Listen, now that you have two good hands, what are your plans? Juggling? Piano? What is it you dream about doing, my friend?"

In my imagination, they chat about this man's long-awaited passion pursuits. And possibly the man then turns to Jesus and says, "Well, what are *your* dreams? I mean, you asked me about mine, and so I guess it's only right that I ask you about yours."

And against the backdrop of him resolving a crippling situation to the dismay of a few legalistic leaders, I imagine Jesus articulating his dream with words that are absolutely captivating to me:

"You know, I dream that someday, places of worship will be filled with people who lay awake at night concerned about the human beings my Father created. Who care about broken bodies and broken souls and hopeless futures and hell-bound eternities. I dream of the day when people who gather in my name are so filled with the love of the Father that they go out and spread his love and extend healthy hands to withered hands — praying, coaching, and encouraging them to walk in fullness of life. I dream of worship centers filled with radically loving, outwardly focused, Christ-sharing people. *That's* what I dream about."

I have to wonder, is this what you dream of too?

FULFILLING CHRIST'S DREAM

One of the outputs of the management team meeting I mentioned previously was a teaching platform to educate Willow members on how to reach out to people who live near them, regardless of religious affiliation or spiritual beliefs. We encouraged them to start small, with block parties or cookouts or other nonthreatening get-togethers where the fragile relational strands of developing friendships could be woven together.

One particular neighborhood sensed the need to create a neighborhood newsletter that would give voice to every home on their few blocks. It would give everyone a stake in the goings-on of their shared community. Rather than being an explicitly "Christian" or Willow-based piece, it was set up to be a safe and impartial starting point for families to begin uncovering common interests with people living near them.

A Willow person who was heading up this initiative came to church deflated sometime later. "You won't believe this," he told a management team member, "but one of the ladies in our neighborhood wants to put an ad for her tarot card–reading business in our neighborhood newsletter." He was chagrined because his deep desire to build bridges toward Christ was not being fulfilled by the lady's request.

In the end, this Willow person had no choice but to include the ad in the newsletter. Either it was bias-free and religion-free or it wasn't, right?

Christ-followers in all sorts of neighborhoods must make the same bold decision to enfold unbelievers with the care, compassion, and love of Jesus Christ. Because everywhere we turn in this world, we encounter people with withered parts. People with withered minds who find themselves ensnared by psychological scars or sinful thoughts or selfish motives. People with withered hearts who see no purpose in today and have no hope for tomorrow. People with withered bodies who feel encumbered and who struggle to accomplish mundane tasks throughout the day. People with withered souls who don't yet know that there is a God who loves them and who has paved a path for them to know him.

But the astounding truth for you and me is that as we work to develop friendships with anyone and everyone we meet, we just might be the one the Holy Spirit uses to heal some withered hands in our little corners of the world.

STUDY QUESTIONS

1. Which life cycle is truest of your faith journey—the one that starts strong but fizzles out or the one that continues to reflect an ever-increasing amount of radical inclusiveness of all people, regardless of where they are on their spiritual path?

2. Is this life-cycle the one you want to be known for? What steps can you take to grow more toward the model Christ has given us for spreading his grace to a needy world?

3. Can you relate to the "horse trading" concept? Have you ever privately horse-traded away your responsibility in evangelism? If so, what fears or inhibitions caused you to do so?

4. On page 67, you read that "Jesus had a corner on the "potential" market. He had an uncanny ability to look past the obvious flaws in people's lives and envision who they could become if the power of God were released in their lives." What obvious flaws—or "withered parts"—did you have before coming to Christ?

5. Now think about the people in your life who helped point you toward faith along the way. What potential do you think *they* spotted in you before you submitted your life to Christ?

6. On a scale of 1 to 10, with 10 being the best possible, where would you rate yourself in terms of spotting potential in others who are still living far from God?

7. In the list below, which two character traits would help you personally move toward immediately seeing the potential in people that God sees? End your time in prayer, asking God to cultivate these traits in you today.

☐ Love	☐ Patience	☐ Understanding
☐ Compassion	☐ Faith	☐ Tenderness
☐ Mercy	☐ Humility	☐ Optimism
☐ Joy	☐ Self-control	☐ Goodness
☐ Faith	☐ Kindness	☐ Wisdom

CHAPTER 4

Next, Discover Stories

* * * * •

After what had been a long day of back-to-back meetings in downtown Chicago one Tuesday night, I opted to stay inside the Loop until rush hour had passed. I'd promised a friend that I would review his book manuscript, and knowing the traffic would be a bear for a couple of hours, I decided to find a place where I could get some work done before making the drive back to the suburbs.

I walked into the restaurant of a nice hotel. There was a crowded lounge on one side and a busy dining room on the other. As I stood there trying to decide which side would be more conducive to my working, a young couple entered through the main door. They walked up next to me and engaged in their own deliberation about where they should sit. They were chatting and laughing, appearing open to whatever might happen, so I made eye contact with them. "Hey, I've never eaten here," I ventured. "Would you suggest the lounge or the dining room?"

"We've never eaten here either, and we were going to ask you the same thing!"

They both had easygoing smiles and seemed friendly enough. We exchanged first names, and they asked me if I was waiting on someone or if I was there alone. They'd flown in earlier from out of town and were completely unfamiliar with the area. Since I'd been to their city on several occasions, we were off to the races conversationally. We talked about local attractions in their area, what's interesting to do in Chicago, mutually favorite travel destinations, you name it.

The man excused himself after a few minutes to check in at the host stand. When he returned, he offered to get us all something to drink. He said it could be awhile before a table was ready in either room, but why didn't we take a seat at the bar while we waited. Although I thought that sounded like a grand idea, I realized I was probably intruding on a quiet night out for them. "Listen, I'm fine being alone if I'm throwing a wrench in your date," I said.

Have you ever had one of those experiences where people laugh a little too energetically in response to a not-so-funny comment? I registered their reaction for future reference. "Sure, then," I recovered. "Let's grab a drink."

For the next half hour, we covered dozens of topics — their backgrounds, my wife and kids, recreational passions, and more. It was a ball! I thought it interesting that they never asked me what I did for a living, but I would soon discover that maybe that was for the best.

At one point the woman looked at me, serious now, and said, "Bill, it sounds like you're a pretty happy man." She said it with such genuineness and tenderness. Just then, I felt the tug of the Holy Spirit — viscerally I could feel it. *Here's an open door,* he was nudging. *Just walk through it. You've already walked across this restaurant, you've engaged this couple in conversation, you're open, and I'm asking you to walk through this door. Just test the waters to see if they might be ready to talk about something deeper than sports teams and travel destinations.*

In the brief time I'd been with this couple, my heart had expanded toward them. I wondered how life really was for them and whether or not they were fulfilled. I was curious about where they were spiritually and if they were involved in a church somewhere. I had no idea where this conversation was headed, but I secretly hoped I'd be able to say a word for God.

And so I took another small risk. "You know," I said, without any hype or syrup, "I'm one of the happiest people I know. I have a great life.... I love what I do and the people I do it with. I'm blessed with a terrific family and friends. I'm healthy ... optimistic about the future. All in all, I'm a happy camper."

They seemed to be open still. "How about you?" I ventured. "Where does your happiness meter read these days?" I asked the question playfully enough that had they wanted to bail on the conversation, they could have.

The woman didn't hesitate, though her voice was suddenly shaky. "Actually, my meter's reading pretty low at the moment. Our company just laid off three of my closest friends, and it's been a tough go. We've worked together for a long time.... I guess I'm taking things pretty hard."

The man then said that he'd been in an all-day meeting to determine how many more staff people he had to cut in his situation. "It's a painful time for our industry right now, and the turmoil of letting good people go is awful." We talked about what it's like to lose friends to layoffs, and I was deeply moved by their immense concern for their colleagues.

"I'm touched by your care for the people you work with. I just wonder how the two of you are handling all of this," I said. "I mean, it seems like you both have a lot of pressure in your careers. How does it affect your relationship?"

Things got very quiet. Too quiet. They paused a moment too long, and I took my cue. "Look, I'm sorry if this is too heavy for your night out. We can go back to talking beaches, vacations, all that...."

They looked at each other for a second, seeming to strike a nonverbal agreement to "just tell me" something. In my mind, I geared up to absorb details about the enormous marital strife their work stress had caused for them.

Was I ever wrong.

"You should probably know that we're not married," the woman began. I checked my reflexes and realized I hadn't reacted yet. Thankfully, I still appeared to be holding steady as a nonjudging listener.

"We're just good friends. Well, actually," she continued, "we're both gay."

Now, I don't know what you say when someone tells you something like that. But here's one thing I do know: your immediate reaction is going to make or break you. Regardless of how much trust you've forged to that point, if your *initial* response isn't filled with acceptance and compassion, I guarantee you're done. So, despite the fact that her statement had totally blindsided me, I knew I had to foster an elastic framework with this couple. I had to land on some sort of paradigm that could bend and flex to include them too. But how?

Although the entire conversation had moved so quickly to that point, now it was as if life was unfolding in slow motion. While they waited for me to respond, God and I had a quick chat. More the case, I suppose, I shamelessly begged him for help.

911! I screamed in my spirit. *I could use some help down here! You got me into this, and if you tell me that I'm third in line right now to receive an answer from you, I'm here to tell you that that's not good enough! I need some direction, God, and I need it pronto!*

I felt completely ambushed as hyperactive thoughts flooded my mind. Before I could organize them all, a few words fell out of my mouth: "Well, if you want to talk about *that*, we'd better get another round of drinks! This time, on me."

Just then, the host stopped by to tell us a lounge table was available, and to my astonishment, they agreed to continue the conversation there. I will remember the next sixty minutes we spent around that table for a long, long time. It was incredible—divine, even. They obviously needed to open up to someone, and I happened to be in the right place at the right time.

Their pain level was high in so many areas, and as they continued to talk, I thanked God for orchestrating our meeting. They described the painful treatment they received from people they cared deeply about. They elaborated on the sense of isolation they felt at work—knowing coworkers steered clear of them once they discovered the homosexual lifestyle these two were leading.

My mind trailed off as I wondered how they would respond if and when they learned that I was a pastor of a church. As I reengaged in the flow of conversation, I caught the man's eyes for a brief moment and was jolted by how cold and steely they now seemed.

"You know things are bad when your dad won't even talk to you," he said, moving away from the work situation. "And when he does communicate, it's only through the mail. He's a really religious guy, and he writes me letters to tell me what an abomination I am before God and that I'm headed to hell in a handbasket. That's about all he says to me."

That comment prompted my second 911 plea to God. Now I *knew* the stakes were high, and I was staggered by the implications of him finding out I was a "religious type" too. I did *not* want to botch this.

I silently replayed his comments about his dad calling him an abomination and condemning him to hell in a handbasket. *Please, God,* I thought, *please give me some direction and discernment here.* I knew all of the wrong things I could say in this situation, but unfortunately, the right ones eluded me.

How did I get myself into this, anyway? I needed time to think and space to assess how to reengage with compassion and conviction. As soon as he finished his sentence, as if on autopilot, this is what I heard myself say: "Well, I'm probably more religious than you think. But the people who teach me about God say that he has an unconditional sort of love for people of any color, any background, who are fighting any kind of difficulty. What I'm taught is that there is a God who feels *outrageous* compassion for every single person, regardless of their situation. And two words that I carry around with me to remember these things every day are *grace* and *power*. They're significant to me.

"I walk through each day believing that God's grace can cover my shortcomings—and trust me, I have a lot of shortcomings. I also believe that God's power can help me face any challenge that confronts me."

The man looked at me and said, "The only two God-words that float around in my head are *judgment* and *hell*."

My suggestion came slowly. "Why don't you just trade them out?"

The guy sort of chuckled. "Just swap them out? I mean ... can you *do* that?"

"Yep. Just swap them out for a week or two and see what happens," I said. "Look, every time you think *judgment* and *hell*, give yourself an opportunity to think about God differently and just say the words *grace* and *power*. You never know what might unfold."

The woman then looked at him and said, "Guess it couldn't hurt."

Her words hung in the air unchallenged, and mysteriously, the mood supernaturally lightened. Someone walked by and bumped our chairs. Something caught our attention and caused us to laugh. Real life pierced our conversational bubble once again, and I realized for the first time that we had savored nearly an hour of uninterrupted dialogue at that little table.

The host approached us again to ask if we wanted to relocate to a table that had just opened up in the dining room, but knowing how weary they were and the hour's drive I faced, we all agreed to call it a night.

As we gathered our coats and made our way to the door, the woman turned to me and said, "Tonight was extraordinary. Really, you have no idea." She wrapped her arms around me to embrace me. Despite my well-known aversion to hugs, even I detected deep sincerity in her gesture.

The man shook my hand slowly and said, "Thank you so much for talking to us tonight. Let's see, what were those two words again?"

"*Grace* and *power*," I said. "*Grace* and *power*."

"Yeah, *grace* and *power*," he said. "I'll give it a try this week." And with that, they climbed into a cab and left.

· · · · •

Now, before you mull over that story, let me be clear about a few things. At no point during the evening did this couple fall on their knees in submission to Jesus Christ. In fact, I never really had the chance to share the plan of salvation. I didn't invite them to attend Willow, nor did we exchange business cards, because I don't carry them. In fact, it is doubtful I will see this couple again this side of eternity. As far as I know, that evening was my one and only shot. (I tried to silence old tapes from my younger "evangelism training" days—you could probably guess the question that floated through my mind: "But what if their cab gets hit by a garbage truck ten minutes from now?!")

That being said, if we agree that the goal is to somehow introduce people to the God who created them, who loves them, and who longs to save them, then how do you think I did that night?

In case you're grading on a curve, let me toss a few observations into the hopper, maybe inch up my score a point or two.

PROXIMITY POINTS

Ten years ago Mark Mittelberg and I introduced a concept in *Becoming a Contagious Christian* called "The Potential of Close Proximity." In short, it described the fact that even the most "Christlike" Christians on the planet will be totally ineffective unless they get near people who are living far from God.

The reason I revisit that here is because the stakes are too high for us to gloss over the need to be connected with people far from God. It's the only way that relationships get forged, bridges get built, and God opens doors to spiritual conversations. If you're attempting to do the work of evangelism and your life is stuffed with believers, you'll find yourself out of work pretty quickly. What's the point of saving the "already saved"?

In my encounter with the couple, I'd like to think I deserve proximity points for choosing the trendy restaurant over, say, the lobby of Moody Bible Institute, located just around the corner. I certainly could have holed away in a safe, pristine, "Christian" environment instead of risking rubbing shoulders with a few irreligious types. Remember, trend lines show the average Christ-follower growing increasingly isolated from the exact group he or she is called to reach. My decision to head for a bustling restaurant reflected a conscious desire to hang out where people living far from God would also be comfortable hanging out.

Doesn't get much more complicated than that.

Over the years, I've run across a common misconception people have about my credibility to speak to the issue of proximity. People say, "Well, sure, it's easy for *you*. You're a pastor! You're *always* around people who need God." And while it's true that I have opportunities to hear from seekers on occasion who approach me after a weekend service, left to its own devices my life is made up almost entirely of people who are already following Christ.

Those of you who serve in full-time ministry understand that this proximity issue is harder than most people imagine. Within an hour of waking up tomorrow morning, countless friends of mine (and yours) will step foot in an office where they are utterly surrounded by people whose hearts have never received the love of Christ. Others will walk onto a construction site or onto a school campus, through neighborhood streets or local shops or city buildings. And I think, *You lucky dogs! You can experience the great adventure all day, every day!*

I envy those of you who work in the marketplace day in and day out, almost entirely surrounded by people far from God. I covet your never ending proximity to people who would be deeply impacted by your spiritual potency. Not to complain, but for me, getting close to people who need Christ's witness in their lives requires wrenching my whole world out of shape. I have to work hard to stay "out there" in the world and get creative about finding ways to envelop irreligious people in friendship.

This conviction drove the formation of my sailboat racing team I wrote about previously. It wasn't just any sailboat racing team, mind you: I had criteria. Every prospective member had to love sailboat racing, he had to be *good* at sailboat racing, and he had to be living far from God. It was kind of an odd filter, I guess, but the team that resulted from it would take me on the ride of my life!

Several of the original members, along with many of their spouses or girlfriends, came to faith as a result of that team. Over time, another opportunity emerged among those teammates—something that I refer to as "seeker and stray" dinners. These seeker small-group discussions still occur today: every Sunday night that I spend in South Haven includes a two- to three-hour dinner with a few Christ-followers and a couple of people far from God. The purpose is simply to see what God is up to in each other's lives and to stay open to him carving out room for something spiritual in people's hearts.

Living in 3D involves developing friendships with the people right around you—many of whom are living rather far from God. But it doesn't end there. Once you look up, really seeing into those eyes that you encounter day in and day out, the next step is to intentionally discover their stories. Learn what life has been like for them. What they dream about. What is going well in their estimation and what needs work. And as you might guess, these discussions don't occur at arm's length. You have to throw yourself into people's lives to earn the right to have these types of conversations.

POINTS FOR BEING "IN STYLE"

Second, in my humble opinion, I deserve points for staying congruent with my natural style. When I initiated my conversation with the couple, I was operating squarely within my God-given style. I'm mildly extroverted —not totally, but somewhat. I've been told that I have reasonably good social skills. So striking up a conversation with strangers and diving into an interpersonal dialogue is nothing foreign or frightening to me.

But there are certainly things I could have said or done that would *not* have been congruent with my style. You too probably know when you've veered off the road and are freewheeling outside of your comfort, style, or personality lanes. Here's my point: God made you exactly as you are. He wired you and gave you the temperament and the experience and the background that you have because he wanted someone just like *you* in this world right now. Today. In *this* generation. Memorize all twenty-four verses of Psalm 139 if you have to, but don't lose sight of the intentionality God poured into his blueprint for you.

* * * * ●

Scripture is replete with examples of various styles God uses to accomplish his purposes. Peter walked around with his foot perpetually stuck in his mouth. He shot straight—sometimes too straight—with people about his beliefs, giving him the reputation for having a *confrontational* style.

Paul's mental prowess and strong educational training were made manifest in his organized, analytical, and reasoned *intellectual* approach to sharing his faith. His letters reflect an almost legal approach to his arguments, demonstrated by point-counterpoint articulation of truth.

Christ is best known for initiating everyday conversations with his listeners. He relied on parables that used common language and ideas to get his spiritual points across. His *interpersonal* style was accessible to people of all backgrounds, all ages, and all experience levels.

To characterize this you might recall a time when Jesus directed the crowd's attention to a nearby fig tree. The people all craned their necks as he taught a lesson using the tree as a visual aid. While they were all staring up at the tree, a bird landed on its branch. Then he delivered his key lines: "Look at the sparrow there. Not a single sparrow falls without the Father knowing about it and caring for it; every one of you is worth more than the sparrow is worth! God watches over your life, and he loves you." Gene Appel, one of Willow's teaching pastors, has this style in spades, enjoying bottomless cups of coffee and normal, everyday discussions with people as he endeavors to point them toward God.

The woman at the well, whose story we'll explore in part 4, had an *invitational* style, evidenced by her enthusiastic request that her family and friends "come see this man who knew my whole background!" She could hardly contain her excitement over having met the Messiah and wanted nothing more than for everyone else to come to the party she'd happened upon.

Mother Teresa had a *serving* style of evangelism that showed up in her propensity to show Christ's love with actions more than with words.

A modern example of the *testimonial* approach is found in someone like Lee Strobel, who tells the story of his dramatic transformation from antagonistic atheist to devoted Christ-follower in painting a picture of the life change only Christ can enable.

When you interact with people, keep your natural style in mind. As far as I know, God never advised squeezing yourself through a stiff evangelism course or walking around like a hyped-up God-robot with one finger stuck in a socket. But we probably all know people who become evangelistic zealots and start operating incongruently with their God-given style. They talk themselves into believing that they have to be more aggressive, more verbal, more expressive, more dynamic, more whatever, in order to point someone else to Christ. It's just not true.

When the Spirit prompts you to leave a Circle of Comfort, walk across a room, and enter the Zone of the Unknown to discover someone's story, he wants *you* to show up, not someone you think you are supposed to be. Let the conversation ebb and flow in sync with your authentic self.

POINTS FOR PRACTICING COMMONALITY

Ever notice how people light up when you mention something they love? When you're first getting to know people, relax your agenda enough to uncover what they're involved in. The first things I talked about with my "*grace* and *power*" friends were things we would likely have in common, such as entertainment or travel. First Corinthians 9:22 says, "To the weak I became weak, to win the weak. I have become all things to all people so that by all possible means I might save some." In light of Paul's approach, watch for ways to build bridges instead of walls when you are discovering people's stories.

* * * * •

I remember the days when I was pretty green in the whole sailboat racing thing. I walked into a little marina in Michigan one afternoon and saw a gentleman working across the counter who was obviously a boater himself. He just had that look. I'd recently purchased a used sailboat and was interested in racing it, but I had no idea where to begin. So I introduced myself and asked if he'd be willing to explain to me how to do the starting line of a sailboat race.

"Absolutely!" he said as he proceeded to sketch it out. Without seeming too mystical, I truly sensed an open door with this guy. For whatever reason, I had the distinct feeling that we would have lots of conversations in the future.

As I was leaving that day, I asked him if he would consider joining me on the boat sometime to help me sort out the racing thing. "I'm pretty uninformed," I admitted.

"I'd love to!" he said.

And to make a long (and remarkable) story short, several years and hundreds of incredible, God-ordained conversations later, he chose to give his life to Christ. Soon after, he was baptized in the lake just outside of Willow's auditorium. A few years later, he had found and married a Christian woman, had two little girls, and was plugged into a thriving Willow Creek Association church on the other side of town, a church that is now growing by leaps and bounds.

Not to oversimplify, but his entire life transformation can be traced back to one simple conversation across a tiny marina counter. That's where it all began. Based on my experience, most people who wind up in the kingdom of God can trace their salvation back to a single, life-changing conversation with a Christ-follower. *This* is the power of staying the course until you uncover mutual interests with the people you're talking to. God just might use those eight minutes of dialogue to alter a person's eternity.

HIGH MARKS FOR THE SENSITIVITY ATTEMPTS

If I haven't justified a solid score in your eyes yet, let me try this one on you. Remember when the woman offered an observation about how happy I seemed? Perhaps she was fishing for me to elaborate; I don't know. But I knew this much: my reply to her could have easily shut down the conversation right there.

What if when she said, "Bill, it sounds like you're a pretty happy man," I'd spouted off with, "Well, yes I am! I have unbounded happiness because I possess eternal life in Jesus Christ, my Lord and Savior. Moreover, if you accept him right now, *you* can be this happy too!"

Come on now. Her eyes would have glazed over, and her jaw would have dropped into the bread basket. My response was deliberate — I wanted to keep all doors open. My follow-up was also deliberate — as quickly as possible, I positioned the spotlight back on her by asking a couple of questions: "How about you? Where does your happiness meter read these days?" I wasn't looking for a specific answer; I was simply trying to seize every opportunity to get to know her better. The goal was to discover *her* story, not to drone on about mine.

Similarly, to cycle back to an issue that is bound to be on some of your minds, allow me to address how I responded to the couple's sexual orientation. The minute you read that part of the episode, some of you probably thought, *You know, Bill, I'm a little disappointed in you. Here you're given a prime opportunity to confront their disobedient and dishonoring sexual patterns, and it looks to me like you sheepishly skirted the issue altogether.*

If that's true for you, I certainly understand. In the moments I had with that couple, I *shared* your concern. But here's my thinking on the matter: as I've conveyed, I believe the highest value in personal evangelism is to be attuned to the movement and prompting of the Holy Spirit and to play only the role you are intended to play in another person's life. Second to that value (and it's a close second) is being *radically inclusive* of where people are when you find them. Not recklessly condoning the sins they confess, but rather accepting them just as they are.

If these situations make you uncomfortable, join the club. If it weren't for God's grace, I'd capsize trying to navigate turbulent waters like those each and every time. In the midst of controversial issues, I'm never quite sure what to say or do — which explains my double-whammy 911 plea to God. But when I'm staring directly into the eyes of someone living far from God, I'm reminded that my singular focus must be on their *ultimate* issue, which is what they are going to do with the person of Jesus Christ. To use imagery you may now appreciate, my goal was not to expose all the ways their hands were withered so much as to help them see that healing can be theirs.

Based on my understanding of Scripture, this is how Jesus responded to people too. He didn't expect people who had lived their entire lives far from God to be holy when he encountered them. What was of utmost importance to Jesus was that irreligious people were willing for him to *make* them holy. It didn't matter where they had been or what they had done; the "irreligious" types whom Jesus befriended were drunks and thieves and liars and adulterers and egomaniacs and extortionists and a combination of all sorts of things. But to Christ, what mattered more than where they came from was the direction in which they were headed.

It was true for me, at least. Jesus befriended me when I was seventeen years old. Me—a cocky, rebellious, high-risk, thrill-seeking know-it-all who desperately needed him. And guess how holy Christ expected me to be when he found me? You got it. He started with me right where I was. Hopefully, we didn't stay there: hopefully, we've made progress along the way. But thankfully, he embraced me right where I was.

And thankfully, if you are a Christ-follower, he started with *you* right where you were. Right?

These days, my mantra is one I think Jesus himself used: Anyone, anywhere. That's it—anyone, anywhere, can be transformed into a new creation through the power and grace of our Lord. Every morning, I commit myself afresh to staying attuned to the Spirit. I try to pour out huge amounts of radically accepting love as I discover people's stories. I try to walk with people from where they are today toward Christ, trusting that along the way we'll click off all of the patterns of unrighteousness that need to be clicked off for them to be conformed to Christ's image.

TAKE THE RISK!

All right, by now I hope you've come to your own conclusion about how I did. Frankly, I'll take whatever score you give me, as long as you don't miss the point of the story. As Christ's followers, we're accountable for regularly moving in circles with people far from God, uncovering their stories with compassion and grace, and then naturally and consistently making ourselves available when God opens a door of opportunity. People living far from God need the redemption and strength and stability that you can offer—just as you did before you came to Christ.

Since that evening in downtown Chicago, I've often wondered whether they took me up on the noun exchange I offered them. I've wondered whether other Christ-followers worked to get some proximity with this couple in order to water the small seed I planted. What is important to me is the assurance that I played only the role I was intended to play that night. And the rest of the story is up to God to write. For me, *that* is what it's like on the exciting, Spirit-led edge of life!

To shoot straight, I have to admit that this "exciting edge" always involves discovering stories of *real* people living *real* lives. As I experienced with my "*grace* and *power*" friends, there will be uncomfortable moments. There will be messy realities. And some cases will require emotional heavy-lifting, because as the Holy Spirit moves in people's hearts, sins and failures they've racked up over time tend to surface.

Some time ago, I was pulling out of our parking lot after one of our midweek services. I had a meeting following the service, and I remember it being very late at night. Out of the corner of my eye as I was about to pull onto Algonquin Road, I noticed a man standing beside his car on the edge of the lot, his arms hugging his chest as if to brace himself against the bitter cold.

It was pitch-black outside, and although I was surprised to have noticed him at all, it paled in comparison to the surprise I would discover seconds later. I felt an undeniable prompting to circle back into the lot and see if I could be of help.

The day had been impossibly long, but the Spirit was guiding me. After turning my car around, I pulled up next to him and stepped out into the shadows.

"Are you ... okay?" He looked up, realized who I was, and immediately fell apart. *Oh, man, what have I just walked into?* I tried to settle him, but his inconsolable bawling only seemed to escalate.

"You won't believe this," he sort of whimpered through his tears, each syllable interrupted by long pauses, "but earlier today, I paid for a woman's abortion. I can't live with the guilt that has come into my heart. It's too much to bear. It's just too much! I sat through that service tonight, feeling such immense guilt." His gut-wrenching agony showed up in big pools of tears. "It's like *I* killed her baby. I killed our baby!" He kept repeating the reality of his situation, over and over and over again. I couldn't get past the intense pain this would-be father felt, the paralyzing culpability he was experiencing. My heart broke for him.

I felt completely disoriented—this territory was totally unfamiliar to me. Treading very, very carefully, I agreed as gently as possible that he had made a dreadful mistake. I knew it would be jolting to him for me to acknowledge this, but it was better than trying to paint a happy face on the situation. He was well aware that he'd made a horrible decision; the guilt was written all over his face, his pain dripping down in every tear he cried.

After several minutes, he finally began to calm down. Our conversation slowly resumed. I didn't skim over the seriousness of what he had done, but I was extremely careful not to torment him further by rubbing his face in his sin. Every time I'm confronted with the depravity of someone else's sin, all I can think about is my own fallen state and my own proneness to fall short of God's standard. But equally true is the other thing that comes to mind: Jesus Christ's response to my sorry state was acceptance rather than condemnation. His posture toward me when I was in the midst of my sin was filled to the brim with compassion, grace, tenderness, and mercy.

On that night, I believed my role in this man's life was to reflect Christ's love and understanding, and then to allow space for the Holy Spirit to convict of sin.

"Have you had time yet to apologize to God for what you've done?" I asked him.

We prayed together and then agreed that he needed to apologize to the woman and to figure out how to make appropriate amends with her. That night, standing in the darkness of a barren parking lot, a broken man reopened his heart to God and began what would be a long and painful journey toward being put back together again.

Whenever I recall that night, I am reminded of the undeniable power of grace. For the rest of his days, one sin-scarred soul would likely remember a few holy moments shared in a church parking lot, when he faced his sin head-on and found forgiveness through Christ.

I know I will.

Friends, there is no question in my mind about whether these encounters are worth it, even the messiest of them. I challenge you to take the risk to sideline your own agenda and discover other people's stories no matter how uncomfortable you get, how awkward the situation becomes, or how heavy the sin is that you're sorting through with them. Why? Because you just might be the single flame in someone's dark night who reminds them that there is a God who created them, who loves them, and who yearns to relate with them, starting from right where they are.

STUDY QUESTIONS

1. Which area of effectiveness do you practice most in your interactions with people far from God?

    ☐ Proximity — choosing to traffic where seekers traffic

    ☐ Staying in style — trusting God to use your natural personality

    ☐ Practicing commonality — watching for ways to build bridges instead of walls

    ☐ Being sensitive — remembering that irreligious people won't be very holy when you find them

2. Which "evangelistic style" below most closely reflects your own? Please explain. See pages 85–86 for examples of each style.

    ☐ Confrontational

    ☐ Intellectual

    ☐ Interpersonal

    ☐ Invitational

    ☐ Serving

    ☐ Testimonial

    ☐ Other: _____

3. Think about your present sphere of influence — including where you live, where you work, the people in your small group, your friends, your relatives, your acquaintances, and so on. How do you think God expects *your* specific evangelistic style to impact the lives of these people?

4. What is one action item you can accomplish this week that will cause you to use your evangelistic style in discovering another person's story?

5. Have you ever encountered someone's "messy reality" as described in the story beginning on page 90? What was the experience like? Based on this reality, why do you suppose it is so important to listen for the Holy Spirit's guidance in *all* evangelistic situations?

CHAPTER 5

Finally, Discern Next Steps

During a Super Bowl party a few years ago, I got into an interesting conversation with a gentleman I'd never met before. Just as the halftime show was ending, he started opening up about some deep issues. I got the sense that something supernatural was happening, but as the room began to buzz again with excitement for the second half, everyone's attention was refocused on the giant screen in front of us. It wasn't exactly an opportune time to pull him off to the side and start in on the Sinner's Prayer.

I took inventory of my motivations, realizing that all I really wanted to do was serve him. I didn't have lofty notions of being the one to help him cross the line of faith right then and there. Nor was I expecting an offer from him to skip the second half and hole away so that we could hash through the essential doctrines of Christianity. I knew he wanted to see the game (as did I), but I also knew our interaction was not accidental.

Before we rejoined the crowd, I asked if there was any way I could serve him in his spiritual quest—anything he could think of that I might do to help.

His answer was heartfelt. "If you wouldn't mind, pray that I'd be able to understand this faith thing more."

"Of course," I agreed. "And if anything else comes to mind, I hope you'll let me know."

He then admitted that he'd never read a "Christian" book but said that if I'd send him something, he'd read *one* chapter. "But only one!" he added. The good-natured grin on his face told me that his restriction was only half-serious, but I took him up on the challenge.

As soon as I returned home, I stared at the book spines on my library shelves, trying to figure out which book to send, knowing I had only a single chapter to work with. One shot!

I prayed as I scanned the shelves, my adrenaline pumping. *Father, direct me to the right book. Take my preferences out of the equation altogether.... This is all about him. Just show me what it is that you want him to read. Lead me to the right book, and I'll make sure he receives it.*

THE RIGHT RESOURCES AT THE RIGHT TIME

Days later, the book finally in his hands, I reflected on the experience. There was a period in my life when the exchange would have left me feeling like a salesman whose face had met a slammed door. But not this time.

This time, I felt completely at peace about the way our conversation had unfolded at the party. And equally content regarding the abrupt stopping point. As I continued to reflect, I realized that over the years, time and experience had dramatically shifted my perspective. At some point, I'd figured out that despite all of the *potential* roles I could play in evangelistic situations, I consistently gravitated toward one role in particular—that of Resource Provider.

Resource Providers are servant-minded people who make a habit of uncovering the needs around them and then meeting them as naturally and effectively as possible. A Resource Provider is *not* a Salvationist for wayward types, the moral conscience for stragglers and strays, or a Bible Answer Man wannabe. Just a humble man or woman looking to help point people toward God.

THE THIRD *D*

In chapters 3 and 4, we looked at the first two aspects of what it means to "live in 3D." If you want to become a walk-across-the-room person, then you will choose to Develop friendships with people in your world and then take risks to Discover their stories. In this chapter, I'll cover the third *D*—learning how to Discern appropriate next steps.

Next steps—the ones that follow those steps that took you across the room in the first place. The ones that tend to be risky, but in a calculated sort of way—because the Spirit is guiding. So although Christ-followers never know exactly how next steps will be received, they continue to risk testing a few, acknowledging that spiritual ground will never be gained otherwise.

·   ·   ·   ·   •

Suppose you're at a cocktail party. You take the risk to approach someone who is standing alone, and you strike up a conversation. You then gather some interesting facets of their story. But will you go a step further and ask a couple of deeper questions about their journey, or will you let things stay superficial and then make a joke to ease the discomfort of your exit as you walk away?

Or perhaps you're returning from a business trip, and halfway into the flight the man seated next to you feels comfortable enough in your conversation to mention he's still reeling from the death of his dad earlier in the year. You remember a book you once read that solidified your own faith after you had walked through a significant season of grief. Will you take the risk to reveal your belief in God and recommend the book, or will you give him a sympathetic nod and then migrate to a different subject?

Standing in your child's classroom at the school holiday party, you overhear the teacher telling another parent that this month will be a little tough since she won't be able to make the trip back east to spend Christmas with her family. Alone for the holidays ... not good. Will you risk inviting her to Christmas Eve services with your family or to your home for a leftovers party after Christmas, or will you act as though you never heard about her situation?

In your day-to-day life, there are countless opportunities where forks in the road like these show up. Situations where you have to declare to yourself and to God whether or not you will take the next step to have impact in people's lives. Here's the bottom line: choosing wisely in these fork-in-the-road moments is what becoming a Resource Provider is all about.

You don't have to be any more talented, any richer, any slimmer, any smarter, any more or less of *anything* to partner with God. All you have to be is willing to be used by him in everyday ways. If that's true of you, then let's get all over this assignment of learning to discern appropriate next steps in pointing people toward him!

INITIAL INTERACTIONS

I have a friend whose family recently relocated to a new city. A few days after moving in, she met her next-door neighbor. During their brief exchange, the neighbor volunteered a few details about her life: she had four kids and a husband, worked at a large corporation, and struggled to get the work-and-home balance right. Her oldest son—a strong-willed eighteen-year-old, according to her—was waffling about whether or not to go to college and was working as a sacker at the nearby grocery store.

Her family constantly juggled dozens of overlapping activities like baseball games and her husband's business trips, causing their two Labrador retrievers to hang out in the backyard for days on end without attention. After a few minutes of chatter, the two women turned to head toward their respective homes. The dogs ran toward them from the deck, both with tennis balls in their jowls and pleading eyes. "See, this is what I mean," the neighbor said. "They have *way* more energy than our family has time to exhaust. We feel so guilty!" As she walked away, she let out a frustrated laugh that acknowledged the maddening busyness of life.

Now maybe after an encounter like that, you'd politely nod and smile and excuse yourself with, "Well, it was nice to meet you." But what I want you to see is that any typical ten-minute exchange can unearth *dozens* of ways for you to help source the needs of people in your sphere of influence.

Try to catch the crystal-clear signals people send—often unintentionally—that inform you about their needs and that can guide you toward the right resources to suggest. It doesn't take a genius to discern appropriate next steps in relationships. All it takes is radar that's simultaneously tracking the Holy Spirit's promptings as well as the needs of the person you are talking to.

Maybe it's a timely word or a well-intentioned question. A thoughtfully chosen book or message or a fitting seminar or event. A willing spirit, a heartfelt laugh, a safe ear, or—as my work-from-home friend discovered—

a commitment to taking a couple of dogs on a run a few afternoons a week while the family tends to their to-dos. Who knows where that small, caring act might lead!

It really is true—everyday, seemingly insignificant things can become divine, life-altering tools in the hands of compassionate Christ-followers. But you'll never know their impact until you offer them up as resources to meet the needs around you.

*   *   *   *   •

I had been on the road for a series *of speaking engagements one winter when* I decided to head out alone to eat breakfast and to spend a few minutes being still before God. It was blustery and cold that morning, but I remember feeling warmed by God's presence while I whispered a prayer as I crossed the street to enter the café. *Just for today, God, I will do whatever you ask me to do. Just for today.* I didn't want to overpromise and underdeliver, so I took the safe route. Figured I would keep the bar low. "One day. Whatever you ask, God." That was the deal.

A hot meal, several cups of coffee, and forty-five minutes later, I was walking back toward my car, bracing against the blowing snow that was pounding my face. Almost audibly, I received a prompting from God. (These don't necessarily flow into my life in a steady stream, but on that particular day, it happened.) "Turn around," he prompted.

So, as you might expect, I kept right on walking.

To my dismay, his voice wasn't subdued by my obstinacy. "Turn around," he prompted again. My short-term memory indicted me as I remembered that less than one hour prior, I had promised God that I would be available to him for that entire day. How could I refuse his leading so soon after I'd made such a clear commitment?

I turned to look behind me and saw absolutely nothing there. "See, God?" I sort of sneered. But as I wheeled back around, I saw an elderly woman—probably at least eighty-five—who had been dropped off by a city bus on the corner a few feet in front of me. She was out to take care of some shopping but was obviously stymied by a tall snowbank blockading the entrance to the first store on her list of stops.

"How are you going to get over that snowbank?" My tone told her that I expected to help out.

"It's gonna be tough unless you help me, sonny," she said without missing a beat. Looking down the street a little, I noticed that the snowy obstacle outlined the sidewalk for blocks. I kicked the snow bank down some and found inches-thick ice underneath. Even clutching my arm, there was no way she could step across the bank without slipping.

"Ma'am, I'm not sure how to tell you this, but the only way I can help you is to lift you over this thing."

She paused for a moment. "Well I can't stay *here* all day! Lift away, but you'd better be careful with me." She loosened her posture as an early sign that she was ready to trust a complete stranger.

As gently as I could, I lifted her over the snowbank, set her down just outside the store entrance, and then asked about her transportation once she had finished her errands. "I'll be just fine, sonny," she said with a frail hand on my shoulder. "Thank you for helping me. You're a nice young man."

I watched her enter the store and continued heading toward my car, still shivering from the wind. It occurred to me as I drove toward the location of my first speaking engagement that the simple act of meeting someone's immediate need that morning would likely trump the more public and intellectually stimulating events of my day. During a few moments at a stoplight, now in the heated comfort of my car, I speculated about how it all unfolded.

Here was God sitting up there observing one of his fragile and aging daughters who needed help on a frigid winter morning. He knew of this semipliable, strapping (if I do say so myself) young son who was in the same vicinity. And so he sent a message through the Spirit to alert the son to the need. Sure, it got goofed up and ignored along the way, but finally it came through loud and clear. "Turn around!" he had urged. And finally I had turned around.

In a nutshell, that was the extent of what happened that day. God chose to use me to meet a practical need. And despite its evident simplicity, it served to reaffirm my daily goal as a follower of Christ—to be acutely aware of God's activity in this world and to be willing for him to use me in accomplishing some part of it, be it large or small.

Obviously, I have no idea if that minuscule act of kindness played any role whatsoever in that woman eventually coming to faith in God. Maybe she was already a Christ-follower; I don't know. But the key is to have a willing spirit, an open heart, and a mind-set that says, "If there is absolutely *any* resource I can provide that will ease your burden, untangle your confusion, or solidify your trust in the God who built you and loves you, then I hope you'll let me provide it."

BECOMING A RESOURCE PROVIDER

This approach works well: if I view myself as a Resource Provider, I tend to relax in the fact that a person's faith journey is just that—a journey. It's not a box to be checked, a one-time prayer to be prayed, or a contract to be signed. It's a *process* that continuously allows for questions like, "Are you open to some coaching in this particular area?" or "Can I put a good Christian CD in your mailbox tonight? I think you'll love it."

Once I crack the ice in any given conversation, I try to focus my attention on *anything* they might say or do that tells me they might be open to some resource at my disposal. For instance, if I gingerly ask about their spiritual life and they admit to being confused, I look for ways to coach them toward God, one small step at a time. "I certainly don't have all of the answers," I might say. "Believe me, I'm still dazed and confused about much of life, but there are a few things I'm sure of. And if you are open to a little bit of assistance, or if there are any resources that would be useful to you, let me know. Maybe a book or a tape, maybe hearing some of my story or understanding more about God's story. Just tell me what would be helpful."

And if my offer goes unaccepted, I am perfectly fine. Want to know why? Because I can wait them out! Something just might unfold in that person's life when they will say to themselves, *You know what? I think I'll take him up on his offer if it still stands. I think I could use a little coaching, a little advice, maybe some encouragement.*

Then I get to spring into action! I get to reap the fruit of being a patient companion. I get to serve as a conduit, providing whatever resource makes sense at the time. And over the years, I've had the privilege of offering up a wide variety of resources. Sometimes it's as simple as a book or a CD, as I've mentioned. But other times, the most effective resource I could provide to a friend was an introduction to someone who had recently gone through the same illness, predicament, or loss as he or she had. When you're dealt a tough blow, it's so comforting to know you're not alone. It is incredibly reassuring to realize that other men and women have walked through the same darkness you find yourself walking through, isn't it?

Each time I've been present when the bottom has fallen out of a friend's life, I've thanked God profusely that I stayed the course. I've rejoiced that I was able to provide resources that inched them one step closer toward faith, and that patience — instead of some forced agenda — prevailed.

You want the same to be true of your experience someday, right? Believe me, it's not only possible — it's *probable*, if you take seriously this role of becoming a Resource Provider in the life of everyone you come across. If you're lucky, a few of those initial interactions, like jogging with a neighbor's dog or assisting someone over a snowbank, will be marked for longer-term involvement. But here's where the edge comes in: you never really know where things will lead until you take that initial risk to engage. On some occasions, it's as if God whispers a hint of hope to you as you interact with certain people: "Stick around a little while — this relationship will grow if you tend it...."

So how do you move from initial interactions to really making a significant difference in people's lives?

Glad you asked.

THE "BE WITH" FACTOR

At a Willow Creek leadership retreat a number of years ago, I introduced something called the "be with" factor in summarizing Jesus' approach to having the most significant impact on the people in his world. Jesus most profoundly influenced his disciples by doing life with them. He invited them into his world, and he got into theirs. Undeniably, the disciples' most momentous life-change happened during their *mundane*, *everyday* times with their Lord.

The "be with" factor is a concept that's foundational to understanding biblical community among believers, as well as learning how to discern next steps in the lives of people who don't yet know God. You have to *be with* people in order to know what resources to provide. Once they know you're in it for the long haul, they'll allow you to suggest almost any reasonable resource to aid their spiritual growth.

Are you committed to *being with* the members of your various social groups—doing life with them, sharing yourself with them, rubbing shoulders with them?[4] If not, what's holding you back? Christ modeled the life we're intended to live—one that involves relating with each other deeply, earnestly, and authentically. And friendships that are strong today can always be traced back to that first conversation when someone chose to engage, someone chose to seek out the other person's story, and someone was willing to pay attention to occasions when the right resources would meet a few needs.

·   ·   ·   ·   •

A Christ-follower named Anne once decided to get serious about being with the people in her life—specifically, those who lived in her neighborhood. She chose to host a few local speakers in her home who could share their insight and wisdom on a variety of topics, ranging from how to establish family traditions to how to balance the demands of work with the strains of raising kids. Anne invited all of the women on the surrounding streets. A few occasions of appetizers, drinks, and easygoing conversation later, she had developed solid relationships with most of the women on her block.

The trust she built with those women spread to their families as well. Following the attacks of 9/11, Anne and her two young children headed outside one sunny afternoon, armed with cups of lemonade and a platter of cookies. They walked up and down the block, inviting all of the neighborhood kids—regardless of their families' spiritual journeys—to meet in Anne's garage at a designated hour to say a prayer for the world. She was astounded when families showed up, their kids ready and willing to offer their innocent and simple-phrased prayers to God for America's protection and well-being.

Additionally, she and her husband had been serving for some time with a ministry in Cuba. Each time they make the overseas trip, they let their neighbors know of their goals and a few prayer requests. "Our neighbors' support over the years has blown us away," she said recently. "Whenever we are preparing for a trip, many of them sincerely ask how they can help. On most occasions, my family heads to Cuba with loads of clothes collected by our neighbors, as well as assurance that close friends are thinking of us and fervently praying for us as we travel."

Last year, after returning from one trip, Anne and her husband decided to host an informal get-together in their home so that they could update any neighbors who were interested in their trip. Anne enlisted the help of a Cuban pastor who happened to be in town. He gave a short talk on Cuba's current state of affairs and what Americans might do to alleviate the Communist country's strife. Throughout the afternoon, Anne's family interwove stories and pictures of their recent experiences there. Just imagine the amazing one-on-one conversations that were spurred on by that meeting!

Ten years after her first efforts toward building bridges with her neighbors, she now acknowledges that those initial home meetings were a major contributor to the powerful relationships that were spawned — relationships that have been able to weather some pretty severe storms in those neighbors' lives: illnesses, miscarriages, job transitions, dashed dreams, and expectations of children that never seemed to pan out.

You can imagine how distraught Anne was on the day she and her husband decided that for a whole host of reasons, their family really needed to relocate. All those years of investment down the tubes! She was devastated — that is, until God nudged her with the encouragement that she should pour her energies into finishing well in her current neighborhood. She began praying earnestly for the new family that would move into their home, hoping that they would be able to become the relational "glue" she had been to that street.

The family that finally put an offer on Anne's house and moved in shortly thereafter were all Christ-followers. In anticipation of the transition, Anne put together an ice cream party to welcome the new homeowners and to say good-bye to the neighbors who had become like family during the previous decade.

"Seventy-five people came!" she told me later. "It was a tremendous success. You could just *feel* the warmth and camaraderie in the air, Bill." During the party Anne and her husband took photos of each neighborhood family and presented the finished album to her "replacements" on the street. She says that her family's legacy lives on as that new couple, along with their children, run with the torch of Christ's care and heart of compassion for people in their old neighborhood, gently urging them on, one small step at a time, toward the God who created them and who wants more than anything to relate with them.

JUST SHOW UP

Some of you may have this thought bouncing around in your brain: *I just don't seem to have opportunities in my life like you're describing. I've taken countless walks across rooms, but nothing seems to evolve other than a few pleasantries exchanged, a few minutes of conversation shared. I feel like things are going nowhere!*

If this is true for you, then I challenge you to shake things up in your evangelistic routine. Just like Anne did, commit to focusing on a particular group of people who already run in one of your relational circles. They can be almost anyone, whether it's your business associates, your neighbors, your yoga classmates, the guys who run your local deli or auto body shop, the parents of your kids' friends, whoever. I bet if you think hard enough, you can come up with several people in your world right now who would relish the chance to be enfolded in community.

If you don't see a trend in your life of walks across rooms leading to open doors for you to "be with" those people for the long haul, then start with the people you're already "with" and work on discerning appropriate next steps in those relationships first. Eventually, God might just blow open that perfect door of spiritual opportunity for you.

I remember learning of a Willow staffer named Dave who faced a dilemma that nearly all Christ-followers can relate to. He had the "want to" of personal evangelism but couldn't seem to figure out a context for rubbing shoulders with even the people who lived a stone's throw from his house.

He met with several neighbors in the area who also attended Willow, and together they attempted to craft a plan for caring for their neighbors with the ultimate desire of pointing them toward faith in God. Unfortunately, the group was noncommittal. They didn't want to plan anything formal because they had too much on their plates already. They believed it would take too much energy, add to already bulging work demands, and conflict with their kids' existing activity schedules. As you might imagine, Dave was deflated. "I'm going to be part of the *loser* neighborhood," he jokingly lamented.

Like many of you, Dave wrestled with the desire to submit to Christ's exhortation to serve people around him juxtaposed against the reality that no obvious next steps emerged. Not easily dissuaded, he landed on a plan. Dave approached another man from that initial meeting and issued a challenge: "I bet I can put together a better kickball team than you." His neighbor laughed him off but still took the bait. "You're on!"

The following Sunday at dusk, eight families—totaling about forty people—showed up at the local elementary school's ball field. Dave and his wife and two kids were the de facto leaders (a no-brainer—they owned the kickball) and immediately organized everyone into two teams.

They played a quick game en masse and then let the kids take over the field as the adults hung out on the sidelines, getting to know each other and swapping kid-stories between their sons' and daughters' great plays on the field.

"It's been a year since that first game," Dave recounted recently. "During the summer months, a core team of us met every other Sunday night for these kickball games, and the kids loved it so much that they told all of their friends about it. People would drive by and see dozens of us running around and wonder what was going on.

"The first few months," Dave said, "we averaged sixty-five parents and kids every other Sunday night. People loved it! It was designed as an outreach activity, but people kept coming back because it was ... well, it was just plain fun. We invented rules to keep things interesting: moms and dads were required to kick with their opposite foot. Kids younger than five were always allowed on base, often making our final scores reach figures like 48 to 32. We never played more than three innings at a time, so that people always left wanting more. It was fantastic!

"When winter roared in, we contacted a nearby Parks and Recreation facility to see if they would rent out a gym for our group. I went to the other core families and explained that if all of us ponied up a small sum of money, we could continue to feed our kickball habit. Without an ounce of hesitation, they unanimously agreed to pitch in.

"After the first few months, my wife and I opted to spread the planning responsibilities across the whole group so that everyone would have an equal stake in our get-togethers. We began rotating the coordination duties to two couples each week, and the relationships that bloomed even in the context of *planning* our kickball nights were remarkable! Whenever possible, I intentionally paired a Christ-following couple with an unconvinced couple. As they met prior to Sunday to prepare snacks, make attendee reminder calls, and plan the post-game event, their conversations frequently led to spiritual issues, usually spurred by simple questions like, 'Does your family go to church anywhere?'

"Of course, not every family was available to play every time we gathered, but the group continued to grow and expand—as well as deepen in authentic friendship. Right now, if our entire gang showed up on a Sunday night, there would be more than a hundred and fifty of us!"

The interesting thing about Dave's kickball group is that once they had laid a foundation for relationship, events started popping up all over their calendars. They enjoyed New Year's Eve festivities together. They watched the Super Bowl together. Celebrated Valentine's Day and took spring break trips and enjoyed summertime barbeques with each other's families.

Nine months after their group first convened, just about the time that Willow's new auditorium was slated to open, Dave had an idea. The kickball group wasn't affiliated with a particular church or religious bent; that was the point, after all—reaching out to people regardless of where they were on their faith journey. Still, Dave felt a prompting to extend an official invitation to the entire group to join his family for the Grand Opening revelry.

"I'll never forget one woman's story," Dave told me. "When I invited her to join us for Grand Opening, she said that she and her husband had wanted to go to church for years but never believed they'd feel welcome anywhere. They didn't know the inside scoop on how to be 'part of a church' and were uncomfortable in most spiritual settings because they were so unfamiliar with its rituals, rules, and expectations.

" 'Maybe we'll try your church!' she said. I was delighted—her story was just one of the many miracles our group witnessed that year. Without exception, every single family that was invited to that Grand Opening celebration came to visit Willow. Maybe not that weekend, but eventually they did come. It was incredible!"

Friends, this is not rocket science. A little patience, a little perseverance, and a big dose of being tuned in to the ever-present Spirit of God, and voilà, appropriate next steps occur. Dave says that these days, new families that move into their neighborhood end up visiting the kickball group as a means of plugging in to the community. "Three families recently moved in—all on the same street. "And within a month, all three had come to kickball," he said. "Kind of unusual, but it works!"

·   ·   ·   ·   •

On most "nonkickball" days, Dave and his son could be found in their front yard playing catch or tossing a football. During a particular period, their elderly next-door neighbors' son—a single man in his forties—moved into his parents' home for assistance in treating his progressively worsening case of cancer. It was an especially treacherous cancer that rapidly atrophied his entire muscular system. Mike, the son, needed help accomplishing the most menial tasks: rising from bed, showering each morning, dressing for the day, preparing meals, and so on.

Dave noticed that Mike frequently came outside in good weather to wheel around in his electric wheelchair. Dave often spotted him hanging out smoking cigarettes while watching Dave and his son, Scott, play ball. Over time, Dave got to know Mike really well, learning about his upbringing, his proudest achievements, his aspirations and preferences, and his desires and fears.

"Things eventually got much, much worse for Mike," Dave recalls. "His muscles completely failed him, and he was forced into intensive care because his nonfunctioning diaphragm was curbing his ability to breathe. I knew his parents and him well by that point and was compelled to visit him on several occasions while he was in ICU.

"I'll never forget the Sunday night that my cell phone rang with devastating news. Evidently, Mike's life support system would be turned off the following Thursday, and another neighbor was calling to let me know that Mike's days were numbered. I'd just seen Mike a few hours prior to the call, and although I knew I should drop what I was doing to head to the hospital and tell Mike good-bye, I totally wimped out. I couldn't bear to see him dying.

"The next day, I happened to drive right by the hospital in between business meetings, and I immediately pulled over to phone my wife. 'Come meet me at the hospital so that we can say our good-byes,' I suggested. She was right in the middle of a meeting that she was facilitating. So it was basically up to me—a hundred percent my decision."

Dave knew exactly what he had to do. Here's how he tells the story.

"I remember walking into ICU and finding Mike lying there sound asleep, his breathing regulated by the life support system methodically popping and whirring. He looked so calm, so peaceful, so *other than* the frenetic pace kept by those of us not on life support.

"*Okay, God,* I prayed silently. *Here I am. I showed up, and now nothing is happening. I guess I'll stand here staring at Mike until he wakes up—is that what I should do? I'll just stand here waiting.* My mind was keeping tempo with the rhythm of the machines in the room. *Am I supposed to be here? Am I intruding? Why did I come? There are a million and one places I would rather be than here!*

"I had experienced my own struggle with cancer in years past," Dave said, "and the last thing I wanted to do was stand over a hospital bed watching a friend die of the disease." In the midst of thoughts bouncing around in his head, something outside caught Dave's attention. For nearly thirty minutes, he got lost in the activity occurring on the other side of the hospital window, daydreaming and patiently standing by until Mike awakened.

"As soon as Mike's eyes fluttered and strained open, I hopped into his line of sight. 'No, really, don't get up ...,' I joked. As he smiled the wide smile I had grown so fond of, a nurse entered the room.

"'Who are you?' she said as her eyes cut my way.

"'I'm here for his dance lessons,' I offered. Mike smiled again, and I squeezed his hand to convey a silent word of encouragement.

"Mike had developed his own means of communicating during his hospital stay. His voice was so weak that he could barely manage a whisper. Moreover, he had a breathing tube wedged down his throat that would have made even that a painful process, so we often dialogued with facial expressions and hand squeezes instead of with words.

"I'm not a pastor type," Dave continued as he reflected on that day. "I had no idea what someone was supposed to say in situations like those, as evidenced by my wisecracks. Knowing I was probably asking all the wrong things, I sat down on the edge of Mike's bed, the shallow mattress collapsing into the cold, steel frame beneath. 'Are you scared, man?' I asked. 'What do you think's going on? I mean, do you understand what's going to happen to you this week?' My questions were more for my own therapy than for the sake of conversation. I knew Mike couldn't answer me, but I continued anyway.

" 'Mike, let me ask you this,' I started. 'When they turn all this stuff off, are you going to go to heaven?' I strained my ear toward his lips as he whispered, 'I think so.... I think so.'

"Bill, I had no idea what to do then. I didn't want to question the authenticity of his answer, but I had a strong feeling that he wasn't at all sure about where he was headed come Thursday. I said I thought it'd be good for us to talk about a few things, what heaven's all about and how we know if we're going. I asked him if we could pray together for a couple of minutes to get things squared away about the heaven issue, and Mike agreed. So there we were, Mike stretched out on a sterile hospital bed, me crouched beside him with my palms cupping the tops of his folded hands.

"I would pray a sentence, pause, pray another sentence, pause again, waiting for some verification that Mike both heard and understood what I was saying on his behalf. As I kept going, I noticed a distinct squeezing of my hands when I said something Mike especially resonated with. I prayed for his assurance of salvation. *Squeeze.* I asked God to give him peace about his eternal destination. *Squeeze.* I thanked God that because Mike believed in Jesus as his Lord and Savior, he would spend all of eternity in heaven right beside him. *Long squeeze.*

"It was nearing the end of visitation hours, and I needed to get going. I looked at Mike before I walked out of his room and said, 'Hey, because you're going to heaven, I'm not going to say *good-bye*, you know. I'll say *see you later*. Reserve a good street up there so you, me, and Scott can play catch on day one, okay?'

"I took several steps toward the door and then turned slowly, pausing to see that big grin of Mike's one last time. He mouthed 'Thank you' before he smiled the last smile I would ever see of his. And then I left."

That Thursday, Mike's life support was shut off as scheduled, and he died. During the funeral several days later, Dave reflected on the last encounter he had with Mike. "It was like God audibly said, 'Thanks for just showing up, Dave. Thank you for reacting to a prompting and for showing up. That's all I wanted you to do.' "

The Friday following the funeral, Dave and his wife went next door to grieve with Mike's parents. Friends, family, and other neighbors trickled through the living room, their arms clutching pans of lasagna and vases of flowers.

After everyone else had gone home that evening, Dave sat across from Mike's parents in the stillness of the empty room. He told them of his last visit with Mike. But before he could fill in all of the details, Mike's mom interrupted him, a weary smile unfolding across her face.

"We know, Dave; we know. During our visit with Mike on Wednesday morning — the day before they were to turn off his life support — he wrote on a large pad that the two of you had prayed a big prayer. He wrote, 'Everything's okay now, Mom and Dad,' in large letters. Dave, what exactly did you pray with our son?"

Dave recounted every syllable and every squeeze of that hospital visit, ending his story with, "Your son is definitely in heaven." He looked into the relieved faces of caring parents who wanted nothing more than for their son to spend eternity with God.

○　○　○　○　●

I don't know about you, but I find it very interesting that just as a man named Mike was nearing the end of his time on planet earth, God prompted him to relocate to his folks' house in the suburbs of Chicago. Amazingly, the Spirit of God was simultaneously stirring up a passion in a guy named Dave — also a resident of those suburbs — who wouldn't be easily dissuaded in his mission to connect with the people living on the five or six streets in his immediate area.

It seems plausible to me that because Dave had committed himself to being a Resource Provider in the lives of people around him — caring more about meeting their needs than his own — God chose to involve him in a pretty cool kingdom initiative. In my opinion, *every* Christ-follower — not just guys "like Dave" — must be ready to dive into the lives around them. By being willing to offer a creative way to get families together, or by simply *knowing* the people living in houses twenty feet away from theirs, or by ditching their own agendas so they can go stand by a dying man's bedside, just to make sure he's heaven-bound.

Friends, life is too short—for you and for those you know—for you not to show up. When the Spirit nudges you to walk across a ball field, a parking lot, a hospital room—wherever—take the risk to show up. Then take the risk to do exactly what the Spirit asks you to do, offering up any available resource so that one more person will one day be found playing catch on heaven's streets.

It's the next step that you will never regret.

STUDY QUESTIONS

1. On pages 95–96, you were reminded that "you don't have to be any more talented, any richer, any slimmer, any smarter, any more or less of *anything* to partner with God. All you have to be is willing to be used by him in everyday ways." Why do you suppose this so difficult for most people to believe?

2. Thinking back on the story of the elderly woman who needed to scale a snowbank, consider the following question: How willing are you to have your day interrupted by someone else's need?

   ☐ Very willing! It seems as though God gives me opportunities such as these every single day!

   ☐ Somewhat willing ... but it usually takes me a few moments to adjust to the interruption.

   ☐ Not so willing. This is a tough season of life for me, frankly, and even to get my *own* needs met seems to require Herculean effort.

3. Part of becoming a Resource Provider requires that you focus your attention on anything a person says that reveals a potential need you could meet. What would it look like for you to stay focused on *other people's needs* in conversation?

4. I wrote in this chapter that each time I'm present when a friend hits "rock bottom," I'm so grateful to God that I stayed the course instead of bailing too soon on the relationship. Have you ever "stayed the course" in a relationship and reaped benefits as a result? If so, what was the experience like?

5. Look again at the definition of the "be with" factor in this chapter. In your life right now, who are you "being with"? In other words, which of your friends or family members would testify that you are in it for the long haul with them — relating with them, knowing them, loving them, consistently pointing them toward faith?

6. As "kickball Dave" reflects on his relationship with Mike, what thoughts, feelings, or emotions do you think he experiences? Do you believe you could ever have this type of impact on another person's life? Why or why not?

7. For Dave, providing a hint of community for his neighbors all started with a simple game of kickball. What simple steps might the Holy Spirit be prompting you to take to meet a few needs you see? What will it look like for you to "show up" in the world that is spinning all around you?

PART III

The Power of Story

CHAPTER 6

Your Own Before-and-After

· · · · •

Our affinity for stories begins at an early age, as little kids begging weary parents to "read it again, read it again!" As we become mature, contributing members of society, our childlike fascination with the powerful hero or the magical fairy morphs into a simple desire to enter someone else's reality in hopes of making sense of our own. Stories captivate us with characters who seem so much like us, plot lines that give us fresh eyes to see life around us, vivid descriptions of parts of the world we've never visited, and probing questions that force us to declare what we really believe.

No wonder Jesus boiled down profound wisdom lessons and weighty theological teachings into simple stories. The greatest Storyteller ever to walk the planet, Jesus spun sagas about everything from great banquets to mustard seeds, and from trees that bore fruit to missing sheep and lost coins.

The power of a good story? Jesus was well aware of it.

Some of the most striking and intense stories Jesus told were of people like you and me. "A business owner needed some work done and went out to hire day laborers," he would begin. Or "A woman was standing in her kitchen one day, baking homemade loaves of bread. . . ." Jesus' wide variety of stories became legendary throughout his ministry: The good shepherd's compassion. The rich ruler's eye-of-the-needle revelation. The lost son's plight. The lessons of a shrewd manager. The persistence of a feisty widow. But without exception, his stories all pointed to one thing: God's grander story.

Every person alive today has a story too. And possibly the greatest realization someone can make is this: "*My* story fits into *God's* greater story—and that's the greatest story ever told." When people grasp the magnificent truth that the gospel has direct implications for the meaning of their stories, all sorts of lightbulbs flicker to life:

I can be found like the lost son.

I can be cared for by a Good Shepherd too.

My deepest needs—like the widow's—can actually be met.

I can receive *abundant* life just by exhibiting the tiniest amount of faith.

It's really true: *anyone* can get healed, renewed, transformed, and thrust into abundant life. And as I have said many times before, a significant part of my life's mission is to help people on the front side of the cross to have a vastly different story on the back side of the cross. I want to spend my days helping people encounter the risen Christ and, in doing so, to understand that their story actually makes sense in the context of God's bigger story.

•   •   •   •   •

Suppose you and your unconvinced neighbor have forged a friendship over the last few months. The more you interact, the more open and honest the relationship becomes. You've tested the spiritual waters a few times, and she knows that you are "into" God. One day, she asks you why you're so fired up about God. "Sure, I pray when I'm in a bind," she elaborates. "And I go to church at Christmastime ... but that's about all I need. Why is this stuff so important to you?"

In our little scenario here, I wonder how you would answer her. Do you have a response in mind? Because how you choose to fill the few seconds of air space that follow a question like that equates to what I call a *defining* moment.

Think of it this way: living in 3D plants the seeds for evangelism to take root, but being able to tell an effective story is what bears the fruit. The opposite is also true: you can pour yourself into developing friendships with seekers, discovering what their journeys have been like, even pointing them toward some reasonable resources, and then botch the whole deal by not having your act together on the story side. (Trust me.)

When people living far from God throw open the door and ask sincere questions about your faith, you don't need to freeze up. You also don't need to fire off machine-gun bursts of Scripture verses that make no sense to them. Or jump on a soapbox about how they need to start flying straight. Or launch into any number of unhelpful sermonettes.

Instead, you can train your mind so that your default response exhibits the "radical inclusiveness" we looked at previously. Then, with that heart posture fully engaged, you can learn to tell your story—your simple, personal story that conveys the impact Jesus Christ has had in your life. Who knows? You might just give the Holy Spirit something to work with in drawing that person to God.

Now back to your neighbor. Hypothetically, the question she posed was, "Why are you so fired up about God?" If you can't convey your answer naturally, sincerely, and with clarity in the space of about forty-five seconds, then this chapter is for you.

GOOD STORIES GONE BAD

If I seem a little skeptical about Christ-followers being able to tell their stories effectively and concisely, it's because I am. Following almost every weekend service that I am part of at our church, I hang around with other pastors and leaders to talk with people for as long as they want to talk. On occasion, I have to run out to catch an airplane or fulfill another commitment, but nine times out of ten, you can find me standing in Guest Central, talking one-on-one with a line full of people.

In addition to these interactions, I often frequent local spots where I tend to bump into other Christians. Plus, I travel a fair amount of the year and run into still more people in that context. In each of these arenas, it's quite common for me to engage folks in conversation and, if prompted, to probe where they are in their spiritual journey. "Tell me your story," I'll say. "Free shot ... I'm all ears."

As a result, I've heard hundreds and hundreds of stories. Maybe even thousands. And I must admit, most of the time it's not pretty. Not because people don't have a story to tell or because they are unwilling to tell their stories, but because the manner in which so many tell their stories is so appalling. I can't count how many times I've stood before a well-meaning Christ-follower while he or she stumbled and bumbled through some annoyingly exhausting, circuitous trip down Spiritual Memory Lane. Each time, the same thought floats around in my head: *If I were a person living far from God and had even a tinge of interest in this thing called Christianity, after hearing your story, I think I'd recommit myself to paganism.*

Sounds a bit harsh, but I make no apologies. We all need our bells rung on this one. All of us who bear the name of Christ must improve our ability to communicate our faith stories. Because when they're not carefully thought out and clearly communicated, the results can be hideous.

∘   ∘   ∘   ∘   •

I was approached one time by a guy in an airport who obviously wanted to save my soul. We were trapped in a gate area waiting for our flight. For some reason, I had zero desire to engage with him, but I couldn't find a way to escape. He began to tell me about his intimate relationship with God, and as he chatted on (did he even know I was there?), I wrestled with a dilemma. *Do I tell him that I'm a pastor, or do I let him keep on freewheeling while I pretend to be his next conversion project?* I chose to stay put in my indecision awhile.

He started with a burst of energy. "You are never gonna *believe* this! One night, God woke me up!" The passion and incredulity in his voice signaled the beginning of what was sure to be an interesting tale. "I looked at the alarm clock," he said, "and it said 2:22." The man paused for my response to this eye-opener.

I said, "Wow." Still I was sitting there, indecisive and now increasingly annoyed as he continued.

"And then! The next night! God woke me up in the middle of the night. It was ... 3:33!" He kept going, despite no nonverbal cues from me to do so. "Then!" He nearly choked. "The next night ..."

I interrupted him with no attempt to feign interest. "Let me guess," I ventured, "4:44?"

"How'd you *know*?!" he shouted.

In that moment, I had only one question run through my mind: *Why? Why, oh why, oh why?*

Why do people share this kind of stuff in those delicate, first few minutes of an interaction? Why do they trot out some spiritually freakish thing as the anchor point for a conversation with someone they presume is living far from God? Why?

. . . . •

All of us have what I call a Weird God Story. You know the type: something really mystical happens when nobody else is around, and you attribute it to divine intervention. Even I have a few. (Oh, okay, I'll give you just one.) The Weird God Story I've told most often at Willow involves a night when I arrived home from an international trip many years ago. Lynne was out of town, the kids were gone, and all was quiet.

Just after midnight, I climbed into bed and was drifting off to sleep when I suddenly felt a strong prompting to go check the basement. Overtired from traveling, I ignored the prompting twice. Finally, almost bodily, I sensed a nudge. "Go check the basement!" the silence hollered at me.

So I dragged myself out of bed and plodded downstairs to check the basement. Evidently, the exhaust flue from my furnace had broken away from the chimney, and carbon monoxide was pouring into our basement, rising up throughout the entire house.

Interesting, I thought as I shut off the furnace and opened up a few basement windows.

Sleep, I thought next as I headed back to bed.

The following morning I called the repairman to explain what had happened and to enlist his help in fixing my broken flue. After inspecting everything, he said, "You know, given how cold it was last night, your furnace would have run all night and into the morning if you hadn't shut it off. It would have poured all of that gas into your house, and ... well, you'd probably be dead. Guess it's a good thing God told you to go check your basement."

Weird God Stories. Oddities of life that Christ-followers agree are neither coincidental nor explainable other than in terms of God. We all have them. But in your opinion, do I *really* need to tell my flue story to perfect strangers? Friends, my latest Weird God Story is never the first card I lay down when someone genuinely wants to know why I am a Christian. Can you imagine the conversation? "So, Bill, why are you so passionate about following Christ and going God's way in your life?"

" 'Cause one night—at 2:22—God spoke to me through my furnace!"

No, we don't need to go there right out of the blocks. Here is my plea to you: don't start your faith story with the strangest experience you've ever had with God. Save that for later. Way later.

· · · · •

As if I am not in enough hot water as it is, allow me to offer four more criticisms of faith stories; then I'll shift gears to offer a few coaching points for how to tell your story when someone sincerely wants to know why you're committed to living for God. To be clear, I rejoice in the fact that people want to share their stories. I rejoice in the God who gave them stories to tell in the first place. But when eternity is at stake for our listeners, I argue that we must do a better job of telling them.

CRITICISM #1: LONG-WINDEDNESS

The vast majority of faith stories I hear are way too long. Not to be cruel, but when I sign on to listen to what ought to be a three-minute story (or much less—we'll get to that), I expect my clothing to still be in style when you finish. Pay attention to the other person's body language while you tell your story. Are their eyes darting? Are they slowly crossing their arms and inhaling deeply as you drone on? Or something worse? If so, you've got a problem on your hands (there's my well-developed gift of stating the obvious kicking in).

Keep your story brief and allow your listener the chance to ask a few follow-up questions. Leave them wanting more, and trust God to open up a dialogue if you are meant to say anything further about your journey.

CRITICISM #2: FUZZINESS

The only thing worse than a long story is a long story that is incoherent. Here's a common occurrence: I'll ask, "How did you come to faith in Christ?" And in response, I hear half a dozen plot lines about sixteen main characters. I hear of books they have read and supernatural situations they have experienced and conferences they attended twelve years ago. Aisles they walked. Angels who appeared in their bedroom. Dead relatives they have talked to in the middle of the night.

You get the idea. Friends, keep your stories simple—containing one clear plot line that appropriately conveys the heartbeat of your faith journey. We'll cover how to get this done later in the chapter.

CRITICISM #3: RELIGIONESE

Words like "salvation," "born again," "accepting Jesus," and "personal Lord and Savior" mean very little to people who aren't Christ-followers. I listen to countless stories that sound like they are being told in code/God-talk/religionese.

It takes a lot of work to expunge insider jargon from your story, but it's worth it. High praise from an unbelieving listener sounds like this: "I understood every word you just said."

CRITICISM #4: SUPERIORITY

This last criticism usually launches me into a tirade, I feel so strongly about it. I've been in situations when strangers are telling me their stories and don't yet know that I'm a Christ-follower. A few of their pious remarks or haughty assumptions later, I shut down. They don't care about *me*. The only thing they care about is getting the roles nailed down: they are the ones with their act together, and I'm the pitiable lost person, substandard in countless ways.

There may be no quicker way to send an unbeliever to the hills than to play the piety card. If you want to permanently repulse a person from the things of God, try a little superiority on for size. Works every time.

* * * * •

Before we move on to a few coaching points, please keep one thing in mind: if these criticisms have revealed some angst in your heart about errors you have made when talking with a friend about Christ, there is a way to make amends.

Several people have asked me along the way what they are supposed to do about the mistakes they have made in evangelistic situations. Times when they've pressured someone. When they've blown it. When they've tried to take someone across the faith goal line when God really only wanted them to take someone to the twenty.

My answer's always the same. "How about apologizing to them? I don't know about your circumstances, but my non-Christian friends absolutely love it when I apologize to them."

I was in a sailboat regatta once when our team got ourselves into a very tight situation. A couple of crew members mishandled a maneuver, and a bad word came flying out of my mouth. Perish the thought!

When we had finished the regatta and were cleaning up the boat, I gathered the crew together and said, "Guys, I have to apologize to each one of you. You all know that I am trying—often unsuccessfully—to go God's way with my life and to be someone who follows him and lives out his ways. And you know that I don't always live up to this goal, as evidenced by what I said on the racecourse today. I'm really sorry—would you please forgive me?"

You know what? They get the biggest kick out of my admitting mistakes to them. They *love* to extend grace to me when I ask for it.

If you have made mistakes in your sharing of Christ, go seek out the people you wronged and just say you are sorry. "I tried to run past where the Spirit wanted me to go." Or "I put pressure on you that you didn't need." Or "I bored you. I confused you. I preached. I was arrogant. Please forgive me." Whatever it is, take responsibility for it as a first step toward making amends.

THE BEFORE-AND-AFTER PATTERN

The promise of the gospel's transforming power is that when you come to Christ, your old self is evicted and a new self arrives. When you tell your story, the critical contrast to draw for someone is this: What difference has Christ really made in your life? In other words, what were you like *before* Christ, and now what are you like *after* you've asked Christ to intervene?

Allow me a terrible analogy to drive this point deeper in your consciousness. Suppose a friend you've not seen in six months bumps into you and starts raving about the diet plan she has been on. About all you need to know is whether or not the diet made a difference in her life, right? In other words, did she have more body fat or more weight before? And now does she have less of those things as a result of the diet? If she were to net it out for you, what hard evidence did the diet yield?

Or suppose someone says, "I've been going to a counselor recently. I'm receiving unbelievable help from this person! It's really making a difference." Your first question probably revolves around knowing how the counselor has helped: "What made you decide to go see a counselor, and how are those situations different for you today?" In other words, what before-and-after change has the counselor catalyzed?

The same is true for our Christian experience. When someone opens a conversational door for you by asking why you are so fired up about your relationship with Christ, state as simply as possible what was going on before you met Christ and what has been going on since you began to follow him. Interestingly, your before-and-after does not have to be dramatic. It just has to be brief, focused, coherent — and true.

* * * * ●

In John 9, Jesus is seen traveling along when he's approached by a man described as being blind from birth. Wanting to display God's power by healing him, Jesus spat on the ground, made some mud with the saliva, and put it on the blind man's eyes. "Go," Jesus told him, "wash in the Pool of Siloam." Miraculously, the man went and washed, and he came home seeing.

Imagine how perplexed this man's friends and family members and neighbors were! The man they knew to be blind was blind no more. When they asked him what to make of this Jesus person, do you know what he said? "I was blind. And now I can see."

Or rewind a chapter to John 8. Recall our freshly-washed-with-grace friend who was caught in adultery? Jesus rescued her from the utterly humiliating situation and from the Pharisees' stones. "I refuse to condemn you," Christ said to her. "Instead, I forgive you." And then he encouraged her to walk a new walk.

Despite thousands of life experiences under her belt, what single story do you think that woman told for the rest of her life? I guarantee she didn't parade out some strange story about a furnace flue — "Well, at 2:22 one night ..."

No way! She told everyone she met about that hot, dusty day when a man named Jesus changed everything. "I reached such a low point in my life one time," she might have said, "and I was so filled with shame. I got caught in an incredibly embarrassing situation, and my regret nearly suffocated me. And then I met Jesus Christ, and he gave me a new start. He didn't condemn me. He showed me grace!"

How many times do you think she told that story? Over and over again she probably told her simple, true story of how Jesus made an eternity-altering impression on her world.

·   ·   ·   ·   •

Consider Zacchaeus. Luke 19:2 says that Zacchaeus was a wealthy tax collector living for money. He was a self-proclaimed money monger, but after he had dinner with Jesus Christ, everything changed. On the other side of that meal, Zacchaeus declared that he would pay back every dollar, every cent, that he had stolen and extorted from people, and that he would give half of his net worth to the poor. Do you have a hunch regarding the tale he told in future conversations when someone said, "So, Zacchaeus, what's up with your God thing?"

I can just hear Zacchaeus now: "I'll tell you what happened—it was unbelievable! I fell into a pattern where my whole life was wrapped up in money. The grip of greed was so strong that I couldn't break free. It distorted every relationship I had. But then I met Jesus. And you know what? Jesus set me free from the tyranny of greed. He taught me how to care—really care—about people, particularly the poor. That's what Jesus did for me—he unhooked me from unhealthy habits and got me pointed in a new direction."

You know the question I'm going to ask. How many times do you think Zacchaeus told *that* particular before-and-after story? Yes, hundreds of times. And in my estimation, sharing our stories of Christ's impact in our lives doesn't have to be any more complicated than this.

In the context of dynamic before-and-after stories, what might the apostle Paul have testified? "I was so caught up in self-righteousness," he may have said. "That was my gig. Judging, condemning, hating, killing people, all because they didn't commit themselves to God in the way I thought they should." Paul, as you will recall, was persecuting the people of "the Way," the self-professed Christ-followers of the day.

"But then I met Jesus Christ in a blaze of light on a road to Damascus," Paul might have continued, "and it was there that I realized the full extent of my sin. I stumbled across this thing called grace. I went from self-righteous accuser to recipient of grace."

My own story has captured hours of my attention as I've wrestled with what is the *main* concept to convey to people when they ask why I would be willing to devote my entire life to full-time ministry. As you know, my story involves living with the mistaken notion as a kid that the only way I could gain God's acceptance and his approval was through striving. Mistakenly, I thought that if I could only earn more, merit more, or perform more, then God would be impressed with me.

When people ask me why I am so fired up about God, I tell them this: "There was a time in my life when I was absolutely certain that the only way to gain God's favor was to perform, achieve, and strive. But then I met the Son of God in a powerful way and learned that the only way to gain his favor is to accept his gift of grace. Almost immediately, it brought an overwhelming peace to my soul, an end to my useless striving, and a revolutionary change to my entire world."

On the day when Christ met me, the geological plates of my soul permanently shifted; that's where my passion comes from to help men and women on the front side of the cross have a dramatically different story on the back side—that's about all that I want.

· · · · •

Think this through regarding your own journey: What is the single key concept reflected in your life that is germane to the ear of someone living far from God?

I'm reminded of a friend whom I've tried to coach in this regard. When asked about his story, this is what he says: "My whole life up until the point that I met Jesus Christ was slowly self-destructing. I was caught in this terrible downward spiral of self-destructive behavior. But then I met Christ. He gave me the power to begin to live a healthy and constructive life. And I'm immensely grateful."

As you contemplate your own before-and-after, start conducting your own investigation among Christ-followers. Discover what impact Christ has had on their journeys to get an idea of how to articulate your single greatest "so what" about your walk with Jesus.

Many of you know of Bob Buford, author of books such as *Halftime* and *Finishing Well*. In business contexts I have heard him deliver his story close to a dozen times. Here is what he'll often say: "I was nothing more than a bored rich guy. And then I met Christ. He has moved me from mere success to significance. In my relationship with Christ, I am finally discovering a purpose for my life."

Or think back on Chuck Colson's story. He took the fast track from the White House to a prison cell after the Watergate scandal erupted in the early seventies, remember? One day he was dining in the company of the president; the next day he was kept company only by his guilt. But then he met Christ and to his astonishment found grace.

·   ·   ·   ·   •

For some of you, your entire existence has been marked by fear. You have worn fear like a straitjacket that paralyzes you from flourishing in the freedom Christ intends to give you. But then you met this Jesus, the Liberator, and suddenly confidence began to bloom in your heart.

Maybe some of you were contestants in a lifelong popularity contest. The single-minded goal of your life was to impress other people through image management. But then you met Christ. And now your efforts are focused on serving, on hiddenness, or on living in the freedom that shows up when you cease trying to wow an audience.

Perhaps you know someone who could testify to this: "Before I met Christ, I had this plaguing sense of aloneness. I grew up in a broken and dysfunctional family. My days were spent alone, my nights isolated. But then I met Christ! He actually adopted me into his family, and now I know what it means to be *wanted*, to be cared for, to be loved."

It's as simple as this, friends. Who were you before, and who are you now, as a result of Christ's passionate intervention in your journey?

"I was striving . . . but now I'm grateful."

"I was self-destructive . . . but now I'm healthy."

"Guilty . . . but now liberated."

"Fear-stricken . . . but now confident."

"Despairing . . . but now hopeful!"

It's worth searching your heart and soul to firm up the three-pronged foundation of your story: the key word or concept that describes who you were before you met Christ; the fact that you then came into a relationship with Christ; and the key word or concept that describes who you are after walking with Christ for a time.

.   .   .   .   •

Last year during an evangelism series in our midweek setting, I challenged every person at Willow with a similar assignment. "Between now and next week," I told them, "your job is to write out your story in a hundred words or less." Before they could groan about the hundred-word thing, I explained that my story—the one about my errant belief that I could gain God's acceptance through spiritual striving—contains exactly seventy-nine words. I counted. Takes about forty-five seconds to tell, and I would guess I have told it more than a thousand times.

"An email address is about to pop up on our side screens," I told the congregation that night, "and here is what I am asking you to do: once you finalize your story—in a hundred words or less—I want you to email it to me. If I can't personally evaluate every single one that comes in, I'll enlist the help of a small team to get it done. One way or another, you will receive prompt, candid feedback. If we think your story needs some work, trust me, we will tell you.

"If we have to scroll down for two and a half screens just to get to the point of your story, you'll hear about it. If there is an air of piety or arrogance in your language, just back away from your computer when you see our response hit your inbox. And if it leads with some Weird God Story, I'd suggest not even turning your computer on for a while.

"But if you accomplish the goal—conveying your story in a brief, focused, and compelling way—we'll give you an A and cheer you on to go share it."

The response to that homework assignment was wonderful. Hundreds of Creekers took me up on the offer, proving their desire to get better at sharing God's impact in their lives. The examples that follow are from normal people living normal lives, just trying to go God's way as much as possible. They have experienced pain and frustration and isolation and despair like the rest of us, but they acknowledge Christ's intervention and are able to articulate it in a powerful, succinct way.

As you read through their brief stories, pay attention to the themes that resonate with you the most. At the end of this chapter, you will be asked to get your hundred words or less nailed down too.

"For years, I felt empty. I had a hole that I needed to fill, so I searched for things that could fill that hole: a new house; children, new friends, clothes, a new job.... My emptiness would be filled for a short time, but I never found the 'it' that kept the hole filled. One day I heard a message about having a relationship with Jesus. Once I understood, accepted, and grew in my relationship with him, my emptiness was finally filled—for good. Today, I am no longer searching for things to fill my life."

"I used to look for acceptance. I used drugs and alcohol to make me feel like I was somebody. I thought God had put me here as a cruel joke. But then I met Christ. He got me off of drugs, off of alcohol, and he made me feel worthwhile. I now know what happiness is actually like. The void in my heart is gone. I now know I have many reasons for being here ... one is to share my story to give others hope. My days are no longer miserable; life actually means something to me now."

"I was angry and depressed all my life, thinking that the world revolved around me and I wasn't getting my due. I was cynical and isolated. After finding Christ, though, I felt an amazing love and acceptance for the first time. I began to be liked for who I was by the people around me, and my whole life changed. I came to know the joy of relating authentically with people—opening up with honesty and truthfulness about my life."

"My life was filled with shame and fear. I was all tied up inside and isolated. Loneliness led me to a place of hopelessness. But then I met Jesus. Now I am free from my self-inflicted prison of fear and shame. I am forgiven and loved! I am peaceful about who I am and who God is making me to be. The void inside is now filled with joy—joy in knowing that I am a precious child of God."

"I used to struggle under the burdens of a challenging career, marriage, and growing family. I tried to meet these obligations with my own efforts and sufficiency. As a result, I was stressedout-overworked-frustrated-angry-fearful-insecure-anxious-competitive-and-exhausted ... all the time! The challenges still exist, but Jesus eases my burdens and is sufficient where I am deficient. Now I focus on what matters to God, and he takes care of what matters to me.

I face life calmly and confidently while enjoying God's wisdom and his
undeserved blessings."

You can distill your faith journey in similar fashion. Keep it brief, stay
focused, make it easy to understand, and convey it with a humble and
honest heart. That's all there is to it.

·   ·   ·   ·   ●

Quig Fletcher and Pat McDaniel are two men who have been part of the
Willow family since the early days. They both said I could pick on them
for the purposes of this book, so I offer their stories now as great examples
of formulating a good before-and-after.

Quig has chaired the board of directors meetings at Willow Creek for
more than twenty-five years. But before he became such a faithful part
of our church, we crossed paths at the Bueller YMCA in Palatine, Illinois. He and I played racquetball almost weekly, a habit that led to a deep
friendship.

In those days, Quig wasn't a very religious person by his own admission. He thought that since he couldn't seem to stop sinning, there was no
hope of heaven for him. The first time I crossed that locker room to talk
to him, I had enough collateral in the relationship that he was actually
open to talking about spiritual things. When the time came for me to tell
my story, I remember feeling a little insecure because there was nothing
flashy to it. I wasn't a reformed serial killer. God hadn't had to rehabilitate
me from some thousand-buck-a-day cocaine habit. My story just wasn't
dramatic by most standards.

So I walked Quig through my plain-vanilla journey to faith, and soon
afterward he began attending church—then a small gathering of young
kids who met in a movie theater. Many, many years went by, but one day
at the age of forty-six, he met Christ and his life was radically changed.
Because of the work of the Spirit in his life, Quig no longer saw himself
as career sinner but instead as freshly anointed saint—from hopeless to
heaven-bound.

"Looking back," Quig recently told me, "I probably would have accepted
Jesus Christ much sooner if someone had explained the gospel to me. I
had the heart for it but never really had the opportunity."

Quig has been a serving, volunteering part of Willow ever since. His legacy will be finding the land that Willow Creek Community Church sits on today. People ask how we ended up on the corner of Algonquin and Barrington roads in South Barrington, Illinois, and my answer is the same every time: it's because a talented property developer named Quig Fletcher met Christ at age forty-six, committed himself to serving in the church, and one day hunted it down for us.

Another Willow "lifer," Pat McDaniel, became a friend as a result of a walk across a golf green—ironic since I detest golf. A couple of my buddies coerced me into playing with them one day, and Pat was part of a group of guys I'd never met. I walked across the green and introduced myself, and out of that seemingly insignificant exchange grew an abiding friendship.

One day, I shared my faith story with Pat—again with no flash, no flair, nothing fantastic. But he was intrigued enough to begin coming to church with his wife at the movie theater. After having landed in an emotional spot where he could no longer solve the problems he faced alone, Pat turned to Jesus Christ—the ultimate Problem Solver. His problems didn't go away overnight, but God gave Pat the power to overcome what he was facing. And since that time, he has faithfully served among us as a member of the offering counting team, as part of our board of directors, and as one of the strongest advocates for the poor in Willow's entire congregation. These things will make up a mere fraction of Pat's fruitful legacy.

Was there anything spectacular about walking a few steps across a locker room or across a golf green to share my simple story? Of course not. But God doesn't always need the spectacular to accomplish his purposes. Sometimes all he wants is a guy like me to tell his own unspectacular story. In doing so, the Holy Spirit can then ignite a spark that will one day lead to a miracle in a person's life. The proof is in the stories of these two men, who serve as faithful pillars in a church that has been used to touch the world.

＊　＊　＊　＊　●

Your simple, straightforward before-and-after explanation of Christ's work in your life can have profound impact. It is worth working on. It is worth getting right. It is worth falling on your knees every day to say, "God, if there is an opportunity for me to walk across a room, if there is anybody you would have me talk with about my story, it would serve as the greatest joy in my day."

I promise you this: you will be absolutely amazed by the power of your own story once you have been diligent to hone and shape and refine it. When you communicate your personal faith story with sincerity, you will see supernatural sparks fly as God uses it for his glory and your listener's good. Ready for your turn? Rules are the same: pull out a sheet of paper and get it done in a hundred words or less.

STUDY QUESTIONS

1. Thinking back on this chapter's assumption that everyone loves a good story, what are your favorite Bible stories and why?

2. It seems that most Bible characters were known for their faith. Have you ever been asked about your faith? What response do you usually give when people inquire about your relationship with God?

3. This chapter offers four main criticisms of faith stories. Which one are you most in danger of using?

   ☐ Long-windedness

   ☐ Fuzziness

   ☐ Religionese

   ☐ Superiority

4. Assuming you wrote out your "before-and-after" at the end of the chapter, who can you enlist to serve as your "audience" this week? Tell your faith story to three different people, and have them grade you on the following criteria:

   Brevity (You told your story in the space of 45 to 60 seconds)

   Clarity (You stuck to one key plot line)

   Simplicity (You avoided "religionese")

   Humility (You told your story without a pious or haughty attitude)

CHAPTER 7

God's Good News

* * * * •

As the cool haze dissipated during the early morning hours of May 7, 1954, construction began for a five-mile bridge that would link the upper and lower peninsulas of Michigan. It was quite an achievement since the waters below, called the Mackinac Straits, were previously only served by ferries, often causing travel delays of up to thirty-six hours.

Requiring more than a million steel bolts, 466,300 cubic yards of concrete, 42,000 miles of cable wire, 11,350 workers, and nearly a billion dollars, the engineering feat was finally opened to the public exactly three and a half years of grueling labor later.

I'd say it's a lot of trouble to go to for a single bridge. But throughout history, people have willingly gone to such lengths in undertaking this type of monumental feat. Any guesses why?

The desire to span a chasm is just that great.

People on one cliff want to visit residents on another cliff. Merchants want to reach customers on the other side. Families and friends want access to each other. And since the beginning of time, sensing vast distance separating them, people have been consumed by the desire to somehow get over the chasm separating them from God.

But how? they wondered.

They knew that God was *other.* And so they tended to think of God in lofty and remote terms: Perfect. Holy. Awesome. In their minds, his otherness put a lot of distance between Creator and creation. The implications of this reality were significant: if they weren't even living up to their own standards, and God was "other" than they were, then they figured God's standards must be utterly impossible to reach. *This is going to require Herculean effort if we're ever going to be successful!* they thought.

Over time, faith systems emerged that tried to address the question that was on everyone's mind: *How are we going to reach a holy God?* One approach after another came into vogue, hoping to bridge the gap that existed, but they all had one thing in common: the construction effort to cover the chasm always began on humankind's side.

Everyone seemed to agree that all people had to do to reach God was fly a little straighter, pray a little harder, live more nobly, become more religious, and perform more charitable deeds. The idea was that a person's massive construction efforts amassed during the course of a lifetime could somehow entitle them to proximity with God. *Hopefully*, they thought, *by the end of our lives, we'll have worked our way to the other side where we can enjoy a thriving, vibrant relationship with God for all of eternity.*

Study the religions for yourself. See if you don't agree that not only does every major world religion suggest you attempt to bridge the gap through your own efforts, but also there is no evidence or assurance that you will actually get it done before you die.

Every religion, that is, except one: biblical Christianity.

The Bible says something remarkable about how to bridge the gap between God and man. It says that God saw the chasm that separated immoral men and women like you and me from him. He saw the infinite distance for what it really was — more immense than human beings could ever fathom. God knew that *no* amount of human construction — no amount of bridge work — would ever be enough to span a chasm that wide. So, motivated by love, God took on the chasm-spanning responsibility himself. He laid the foundation. He built a bridge that went the distance in order to reach sinful man. He sent his Son, Jesus Christ, to die on a cross for us — the cross that would serve as the *ultimate* bridge.

It was a lot of trouble to go to for a single bridge. But God's desire to span the chasm was just that great. After hours of grueling labor that demanded Christ's physical blood, sweat, and tears, God declared that his bridge was now open to the public, ready to be crossed by anyone willing to take the walk.

．　．　．　．　●

This is God's story — his remarkable tale of redemption and restoration. And there is no higher honor in life than to be message carriers of the great-

est news known to humanity. Because of what Christ has done, you can confidently tell your friends and family that the bridge they're looking for has already been built! "You can take off your hard hat, drop your trowel, and give up your self-made construction efforts," tell them, "because construction is complete, and God's bridge is ready to be crossed." Friends, the whole reason we're here is so that we can spread this news. *The bridge has already been built.*

All that remains is the question of what they'll do about it. Will they abandon their human construction projects and instead walk across the bridge that God built ... or will they plow ahead with their own bridge-building efforts, hoping and praying that someday it will all be enough?

One approach leads to nothing more than behavior modification. The other leads to inside-out transformation whereby minds change. Habits shift. Relationships flourish. And entire life stories get rewritten because of the unparalleled power of *God's* story.

THE BRIDGE

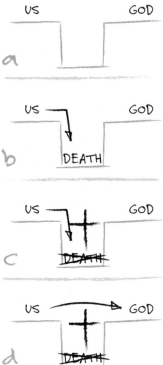

So when you're sensing spiritual openness in a conversation, what's the best way to communicate this life-transforming path? I think pictures work best. On hundreds of occasions, I've relied on one in particular—the "Bridge" illustration—when my unconvinced friends are hoping to understand the significance of Christ's work on the cross.

The explanation is straightforward and easy to memorize: on one side of the bridge is God. On the other side, people. Between God and people is a great chasm, a division that exists because of people's propensity to rebel against God's way and go their own way instead. The Bible calls this "sin."

The dilemma people face is that we want to get to God but know we can't just leap over the chasm. So we try exerting human effort, hoping we can get the bridge built. In the end, we realize that all the human effort in the world will never be enough to get us to the other side. But thankfully, God sympathized with our dilemma. And because he loves us so much, he intervened so that we would have a means of getting close to him. His solution was to choose his Son, Jesus, to serve as the bridge.

·   ·   ·   ·   •

If you remember nothing else about the bridge illustration, remember this: Christ came to earth to be our bridge, and whoever crosses the bridge will live with God forever. The apostle John put it this way in John 5:24: "Very truly I tell you, whoever hears my word and believes him who sent me has eternal life and will not be judged but has crossed over from death to life."

And until the day when you depart from your broken, fractured, earthbound body, you can live with incredible confidence and boldness because, as my colleague Gene Appel says, you know who you are, you know where you are headed, and you know what you're becoming in the process.

The bridge concept has always been meaningful to me personally because, as you'd guess after reading my testimony, Christ found me with hard hat on my head, trowel in hand, and a heart fully prepared to spend every day working on my own construction project. I was seventeen years old when I walked across that bridge, finally comprehending that I could take off my hard hat and let my trowel drop to the concrete floor. God had built a bridge. And by faith, I could walk across that bridge to encounter the face of my Creator.

The truth I discovered as a teenager is the same truth I point people of all ages toward today. No matter what you have done in your past, no matter how far you have wandered, no matter how tightly you have wound yourself around life's axles, God's invitation to you is this: "Drop your trowel and take off the hard hat you've been wearing all this time. Just walk across a bridge that I constructed out of love for you, and once and for all, child, please come home."

DO VERSUS DONE

The simplest illustration I've come across to articulate what sets Christianity apart from other religions is called "Do versus Done." I tell people who are on the Earning-Grace Plan that "religion is spelled D-O. At the end of the day, it's all about whether you *do* enough right things to earn God's favor. To get in God's good graces, the thinking goes, you have to *do* this and *do* that and strive and sacrifice and clean up your act and make all sorts of promises.

"But *Christianity*, on the other hand," I say to people, "is spelled D-O-N-E. The Bible says that what Christ did on the cross is *enough*. He did what you could never do—he uniquely satisfied God's requirement for a perfect sacrifice to take care of our past, present, and future sin—and if you receive what he accomplished, then not only will you be 'in God's good graces,' but your life will be made brand new. Because of what  Christ did on the cross, your sins can be forgiven and you can find favor in God's eyes right here, right now."

Writing those two little words on a slip of paper cements this powerful truth on a person's heart and mind. Whether or not they make a decision for Christ at that moment, they will never forget what sets Christianity apart. The work that must occur to pay for sin and grant eternal access to God—it's already been *done*.

THE MORALITY LADDER

The "Morality Ladder" illustration expresses the universal need for God. If you have friends who don't think they have any real use for God, this one's for you.

Envision morality as escalating rungs on a ladder. God sits at the top of the ladder because he is holy—he's *perfectly* moral. And of course, really evil people are at the bottom—mass murderers and the like. The rest of humanity is somewhere in between. When I draw this for people, I ask them to put a mark somewhere on the ladder that represents where they believe they are, based on what kind of morals they keep.

Before I go any further, though, I toss in a few assumptions. "Mother Teresa," I say, "would probably qualify for a rung about three-fourths of the way up. And just as a guess, Billy Graham probably falls right below her. As far as I'm concerned, I *guarantee* I land lower than those two." I place the initials of the three of us on the ladder, leaving an honorable

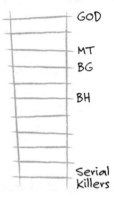

amount of space between BG (Billy Graham) and BH (me). I know my place.

Then I hand over the pen. Inevitably, the person I'm in conversation with writes his or her initials just south of me.

"Okay," I say. "Here's my only question: What is your plan to make up your gap?

"Mother Teresa had a plan for her morality gap," I continue. "It was the cross of Jesus Christ. Billy Graham has a plan for closing the gap between his level of morality and God's standard of perfection. It's the cross of Jesus Christ. So what is your plan? If you believe that you can rise to the standard of God's holiness on a self-improvement program, you will waste the rest of your life in spin cycle. *Real* freedom is found when you ditch your man-made plans and choose instead to accept the work that Jesus did on the cross. You can be forgiven. You can live an abundant life. Your morality gap can be closed once and for all by choosing faith in Christ."

DO YOU BELIEVE THE MESSAGE?

I think that a third grader who has a heart to share the gospel and who cares about people will be successful at evangelism. It's not complicated. In fact, Christ—the ultimate Evangelist—said that all we have to do is to *believe* in the power of the gospel and then *go!* "Take this—the most amazing message ever heard—to people of all races and religions and backgrounds and tribes," he'd say, "and let them know that salvation can be theirs. Live like you believe that this message really can change lives.

"For starters," Jesus might say, "think back on how the power of God's story changed *your* life. Remember that first tug from the Holy Spirit, how you felt when the gospel attached itself to your soul and began transforming you from empty and lifeless to fulfilled and thriving? Now go tell someone about it! Be a purveyor of hope to men and women who need the power of the gospel in their lives."

• • • • •

True confession. Several years ago, I had the privilege of meeting with Billy Graham, the great crusader mentioned previously. During the course of our conversation, I admitted to him that although hundreds of millions of men, women, and children had packed into stadiums and arenas in more than eighty-five countries all over the world to hear him preach during more than four hundred meetings, I in fact had never been to a Billy Graham Crusade.

Not exactly the type of news you want to deliver to someone when that someone is Billy Graham. But there we were, just Billy, me, and the embarrassing truth.

As you might expect, his response was filled with immense warmth and courtesy toward me, the one sorry soul who had never experienced the greatest evangelistic festival on the planet. He graciously made an allowance for my attendance at an upcoming event in San Antonio, Texas. Finally! I'd be able to see one of Billy's crusades live and in person.

I arrived early to walk through the huge arena before the program started, taking in the magnitude of the stage and the endless stripes of empty seats, soon to be filled by the curious and the convinced alike. I was in good spirits, but as the minutes ticked by, I grew increasingly anxious because the workmen had forgotten to place the final chairs on the main floor just in front of the grandiose platform. From where I stood, it looked like they could squeeze nearly a thousand extra chairs in that space — but would they have time to do so before the event began?

(You think I made my confession previously, but the worst was yet to unfold.)

Wanting to be helpful, I walked right up to one of Billy's team members, looked him straight in the eyes, and asked him apprehensively when those chairs were going to get set up (surely it was simply an oversight). I remember his response as if it were yesterday: "Bill, we *never* put chairs there. We'll need all of that space when people come forward to respond to the gospel." He sympathetically patted my shoulder as he walked away.

Yeah, yeah ... of course. I, uh ... I knew that.

After moving on from my humiliation, I thought, *Now that's what it's like to believe*—really *believe*—*in the power of God's story!* Later that same night, when thousands of people were standing in that once-bare area, I marveled at the team's display of confidence in God's message. Absolutely took my breath away.

Do you have the same confidence that God's story really can change lives? While I'm sure many of you do, my unscientific studies reveal a troubling contradiction among Christ-followers in all sorts of churches today. Here it is: although most Christians *say* that the gospel really can renew, save, and transform lives, they get all timid when it comes to living as though it is true. "Um, the gospel? Yeah, it's a good thing for *someone* to talk about with people who are in need of redemption. And it will be *great* if people get saved as a result of hearing God's story. Hope it all works out!"

The Avoiders, I call them. Christ-followers who just keep everything all bottled up. Talk about God's invitation of grace? Not on your life. (Or to save the eternal lives of others, for that matter.)

Avoiders will take a walk across a room, sense God cracking open a door for them to walk through, and then mysteriously fall silent. Someone could come right out and say, "So, tell me about why you live for God ..." and Avoiders will instantly get tangled up in their own insecurities, thinking, *I won't say this right. I've been rejected when I've spoken up before, and I'm not going to do it again. This is just too scary for me.*

Consequently, they shut down. In my opinion, Avoiders take the cake for blowing opportunities to be a witness for Christ in a lost world.

*   *   *   *   •

During the days when Gene Appel was deliberating about whether to join Willow's teaching team, I flew him to our office in South Haven, Michigan, to talk. We spent the better part of the day walking around town, just praying and hashing through what God was up to in his heart and mine regarding the future. Later in the afternoon, a few of my buddies from my infamous seeker-and-stray group called to invite me to go boating. "Come on!" they said. "It's a beautiful day, and we'd all be better off on a boat."

I told Gene that I simply had to say yes; the summer was coming to a close, our sailing days were numbered, and these guys were like family to me.

He didn't dare refuse.

After being anchored at sea, enjoying a few refreshments for a while, the guys discovered that Gene was a pastor from Las Vegas. As if he'd never heard it all before, Gene laughed at the predictable jokes that followed.

But once things settled down again, one of the guys looked at Gene and said, "Seriously now, how does a normal person like you wind up being a pastor type in Las Vegas?"

E. F. Hutton had nothing on the silence that swept across the boat that day. All eyes were on Gene, and even my heart started to pound. Having no idea how Gene would respond, I remember thinking, *With a six-lane entrance ramp like that, if Gene doesn't have the courage to say a word for God, then he's absolutely not our guy.* The thought rushed through my mind with incredible intensity. Even though I hadn't planned it, this boating trip was sizing up to be the ultimate job interview for Gene.

After letting the question sit in the air for a minute or two, Gene calmly and unapologetically explained that when he was a relatively young man, his father had suddenly died. The whole experience had launched Gene into a whirlwind of curiosity and confusion about what existed beyond the grave. Surely life was more than just what we could see and touch in the material world....

"I began to study Christianity," Gene explained, "and I found it absolutely compelling. So I took the risk, opened up my life to Jesus Christ, and found it all very satisfying. The more I grew in my faith, the more I wanted to make it my life's work to tell everyone who was interested that there is a God who loves them.

"So that's how I wound up doing what I do."

When Gene finished his remarks, I sat there wondering how my guys would respond. Despite an ounce of tension in the air, one of them sat back and took in Gene's words. "Cool," he said.

Recently, I was with a friend who had been with Gene and me on the boat that day. He asked how the "priest from Vegas" was doing, and I told him that the Vegas guy was now a Chicago guy.

"You *hired* him?" he asked.

"Yep. Hired him."

"Good. I'm glad you did," he said. "He was a good guy ... really a good guy."

I thought about his assessment sometime after that conversation. The "good guy" label was meaningful, coming from this particular friend. And frankly, he wouldn't have attributed it to Gene if Gene had avoided answering the "God" question. In this friend's estimation, Gene was a "good guy" because he had been real that day. He'd courageously stepped up to the plate, told his story with clarity, and told God's story with confidence and compassion.

Frankly, Gene got it right. He showed courage by being clear about what he believes, and without really knowing how to articulate why, those guys respected him for it.

KEEP SOME SELF-CONTROL HANDY

Avoiders certainly don't do God any favors in the process of evangelism, but they're not alone in their dysfunction. There's another group I've tagged the "Erupters" who are equally disruptive to kingdom-building endeavors.

I feel for Erupters, because their motives are usually pure. At some point, their lives were dramatically and wonderfully upended by the good news, and they got so amped up about God's grace, peace, and all things kingdom-oriented that they simply couldn't contain their enthusiasm any longer.

Erupters live by the creed that it's just *not natural* for Christ-followers to go long stretches of time without telling the story of God's miraculous intervention. They have Romans 1:16 permanently engraved on their eyelids, which says that we are supposed to be *proud* of God's redemptive story. And so they perpetually walk around with an "I've got good news!" expression on their faces.

Most of the time, Erupters live in a constant state of ready-to-burst optimism that someone — *anyone* — will cross their path with whom they

can share the gospel. In anticipation of this moment, Erupters arm themselves with every biblical truth known to man, including chapter and
verse references, cross-references, and Hebrew or Greek transliteration to
boot. They will walk across any room on any day in any city, sometimes
even when they shouldn't. They will take any risk—calculated or not—to
engage someone in conversation about spiritual things.

And all of this seems so good until you lean in a bit closer as the
conversation unfolds. Because once an unconverted person breaches the
perimeter, the Erupter's mission can be articulated in five words: ooze
Christ at any cost.

Rather than listening with a caring and compassionate heart, Erupters
feign attentiveness as they take stock of their spiritual ammunition. Berat-
ing bullets? Check. Sanctimonious shots? Check, check.

Neglecting the fact that the person they are talking to is a magnificent
creation of the most high God, they bypass authentic connection (who has
the time?) and instead tolerate a few seconds of useless small talk while they
initiate the launch sequence for the firing away of their hidden agenda.

Erupters wait … and wait … and wait.

They wait until they just can't wait any longer. And then … look out! At
some cosmically ordained moment, Erupters let loose, spewing rapid-fire
truth all over their stunned victim: "Jesus-is-the-way-and-the-truth-and-
the-life-and-no-one-comes-to-the-Father-except-by-him-and-that-by-defi-
nition-means-YOU-buddy!"

The Erupter's blood pressure rises to unhealthy levels until they get
the verbal burden off their chest. By the time it returns to normal, the
magnificent-creation-of-God person has taken several steps back, thinking, *What in the world just happened here?* (I guarantee you this much:
whatever it was, it had nothing to do with love.) Fundamentally, Erupters
can't display Christ's love when they are in the process of erupting. It's
physically, spiritually, and emotionally impossible.

Maybe you've seen an Erupter in action. Furthermore, maybe you have
been an Erupter at one time or another. My advice to all Erupters is this: if
God prompted you to walk, if he opened the door of conversation, if he has
you standing squarely in the Zone of the Unknown, and if he is arranging
something, then let *him* orchestrate it. Let the Holy Spirit direct the flow
and content of the conversation. Restrain yourself from speeding toward

a point that is incongruent with the rest of the conversation. Remember that redeeming eternities is the Holy Spirit's job, not yours.

I don't know where you show up on this spectrum, where one end is avoiding and one end is erupting. Through the years, I've seen my share of both: Christ-followers who experienced pure paralysis at the prospect of sharing their faith with a seeker, falling silent when things turned God-ward; and believers who were so guilt-ridden about staying silent and standing by as their friends lived out Christless lives that they walked around with a foot perpetually stuffed in their mouth. Either way, I assure you that you can become the type of person who is relaxed, confident, and authentic when hip-deep in a spiritual conversation.

Believe in the power of the gospel, friends. And then commit yourself to learning a few illustrations so that you can tell God's story with passion. The stakes are too high to neglect your role in communicating God's life-giving story to a dying world.

UNBURDENING A BURDENED WORLD

A couple of years ago, while putting the finishing touches on an Easter message, I received word that my mother's only remaining brother had died. Many decades prior, my uncle Jim had been born with Down syndrome and had struggled with the most mundane of tasks each and every day of his life.

As several members of my family boarded a plane headed to Michigan to console my mother and to attend Uncle Jim's funeral, I began daydreaming about the glorious new body he would be fitted for in heaven. What a marvelous improvement it would be! No more pain or suffering or sorrow or defeat. No more challenging days or sleepless nights. Despite the immense sadness over losing Jim in this life, I took great solace in the fact that he would now dance and leap and rejoice effortlessly in the presence of God.

As the jet touched down after our return flight, any comfort I had been given by picturing my uncle in his new residence immediately dissipated. Through a series of telephone calls, we received word that my mother's sister had unexpectedly passed away. Can you imagine the distress my mom must have felt? She hadn't lost a sibling in more than three decades, and now two were gone in a matter of days.

Life felt like a ride on an erratic emotional roller coaster, solace and peace followed by another jolting freefall. Sometime later, I remember reflecting on the sheer shock that death always brings. I know that the death rate has always hovered around 100 percent. But when someone *you* know and love dies, it is inexplicably dreadful. I think we all have a sort of low-grade denial that while death may happen to everyone else, it certainly won't happen to us ... or to those we care about.

Part of what drives this denial, in my opinion, is the ambiguity many people feel about what will happen on the other side. They sort of sidestep thoughts of death because they aren't sure they are ready to meet God. They don't quite grasp the heaven-versus-hell reality and how to land in the right spot. They're nervous about facing whatever reality exists just after they quit breathing. And a little denial goes a long way in helping assuage their fears ... or so they think.

The Bible says that each one of us will face death. It's inevitable. But as Christ-followers know, death is just the stepping-over into eternal union with God, if we so choose. John 3:16 has become rote for many people, but its message continues to shake life's foundation: God so loved the world that he gave his only Son, so that anyone who chooses to believe in him would not perish but would have *eternal life*. You can have it, you can know it, you can be assured of it, and you can be completely confident in it.

I wonder if you know anyone who needs that level of assurance today. If so, then find a way to give it to them!

When the appropriate time comes, I'm convinced you're going to grab that friend, buy him or her a cup of coffee, and begin inching your way through the explanation of the great chasm that exists between people and God. "But he cared enough about you that he gave up his Son—his Son serves as the bridge that gives us access to God," you will explain slowly. "The access—it's a gift called 'grace'—is available to anyone who will accept it and walk across God's bridge. The choice is yours."

You'll feel your heart thumping faster and faster as you measure the weight of each word. But when the moment's just right, you'll say, "You—who you are right here, right now—are worthy of God's unconditional love.

"The same God who created the entire universe also created you and has a purpose for your life. You no longer have to carry your burdens alone. You can lay down your weariness, your sorrow, your suffering, your regret, and your frustration. Because one day you're going to be made new! You will be whole, healthy, complete, and 100 percent satisfied. And until that day, Christ promises to walk with you each and every day, carrying your burdens for you, offering direction toward a significant life, giving substance to your hours and years and life."

At that, you'll probably spot a familiar certain-but-not-so-certain gaze in your friend's eyes. You'll think back on the time you first learned of God's amazing grace, unsure about how to assimilate such life-altering information into your well-established routine. "Take your time," you'll say. "This is a huge decision. But I'm available to help you sort it all out."

.   .   .   .   •

We live in tentative times, but the words of God's story carry weight. The Bible says that the Word of God is alive, active, sharper than a two-edged sword, and profitable to teach truth, rebuke sin, correct errant ways, and train people up in righteousness. So while we face craziness on every level imaginable, we rest in the knowledge that God has provided a path to peace. All people can be rock-solid sure of his presence for all of eternity instead of trembling at the thought of facing a dreadful afterlife.

In heaven's reality, a perfect environment exists, full of rich relationship, beauty, joy, peace, and rest. Just imagine it! There will be no worry about recession, no fear of terrorism, no distress over disease, no confusion, and no chaos. Just perfection—pure, unadulterated perfection.

What a profound honor to speak the words of God's love song into another person's life. And what a day it will be when you finally see your friend, your family member, take those first few baby steps across God's bridge.

Greg Ferguson, a worship leader for one of our weekend teams, once put lyrics to the theme of anticipating the ultimate crossing over—from this life into the next. Let his words sink in as you consider your friends and family members who might want to know that the time has come for them to lay down their hard hats, their trowels, and their self-initiated construction projects. Starting now, they can anticipate an eternity spent with the God who molded them, wired them, created them, purposed them, and will forever love them with an unconditional love.

What a Day It Will Be

GREG FERGUSON

What a day it's gonna be
When at last your captive heart beats free
And all that is within you sings
In heaven's harmony

Sweet release from all your darkest fears
The sound of laughter that's been lost for years
You'll never cry another lonely tear
As your sad heart finally
Finally sings

Hallelujah, what a day it will be.
Hallelujah, what a day it will be!
All those angels that you've never seen
Watching over you behind the scenes
Will at last have reached their goal
Presenting you restored and whole

Just watch the Father laugh and smile
Lifting up his joyful child
And hear the host of heaven sing
In a sweet and soulful angel choir
Singing, hallelujah, what a day it will be.
Hallelujah, what a day it will be!

Here and now in the in-between
We can write it off as an impossible dream
But it's more than a dream to me
Even now I can see enough to believe
I don't know how long it's gonna take
Or how many times our hearts are gonna break but
I'll be walking right along with you
No matter what we have to walk into

But even now if we listen close
We can hear a glimmer of the heavenly host
Hear the sweet holy voices humming
Just a taste of the song that's comin'
Singing, "Hallelujah, what a day it will be!"

STUDY QUESTIONS

1. Do you know beyond a shadow of a doubt that the reason God built a bridge for you was because his desire to span the chasm separating you from him was *just that great*?

   ☐ Yes   ☐ No

2. Choose one or two of the following passages of Scripture to meditate on today. Let them be reminders of God's immense love for you.

Psalm 27:10	Romans 5:5
Psalm 55:22	Romans 5:8
Psalm 71:17–18	Romans 8:35, 38–39
Psalm 147:3	2 Thessalonians 2:16–17

3. Which of the illustrations presented in this chapter most resonates with why you first came to Christ?

   The Bridge—God loved you so much that he asked his Son to serve as a bridge to span the chasm that separated you from him.

   Do versus Done—You don't have to earn your way into God's favor; the work that Christ accomplished on the cross declared payment for your sin "done."

   The Morality Ladder—Despite how good you are, you are far from perfect. The only way to make up your "morality gap," the gap between your standard of living and God's perfect and holy standard, is by relying on the person of Christ.

4. Can you envision yourself sharing one of these illustrations with a friend of yours who is living far from God? What fears or concerns might keep you from doing so?

5. The Avoiders versus the Erupters. Sounds like a low-budget wrestling match, doesn't it? On a scale in which Avoiders are 1 and Erupters are 10, where would you place yourself? How would you define a "happy medium" on the Avoiders/Erupters scale?

When spiritual opportunities arise . . .

I tend to shut down								I tend to spew the truth on people	
1	2	3	4	5	6	7	8	9	10

6. At the close of this chapter, you read that "in heaven's reality, a perfect environment exists, full of rich relationship, beauty, joy, peace, and rest." Think of three of your friends who might be interested in knowing this truth. On a sheet of paper, jot down their names and the reasons why they might want to know this truth. Ask God to reveal ways that you can begin conveying this information to them!

CHAPTER 8

Lessons from the Master

.   .   .   .   .

I was thumbing through a business magazine on a long flight one day and came across a tear-out section near the back that advertised "Lessons from the Masters" videos. You know, Tiger Woods on becoming a great golfer; Pavarotti imparting operatic instruction; Russell Coutts, the helmsperson for the New Zealand team that took the America's Cup, divulging success secrets for sailboat racing.

The marketing hype promised unparalleled results. "Remove previously insurmountable obstacles from your path.... Achieve your loftiest goals today!" Just pennies a day would help me avoid embarrassing mistakes, build confidence for participating in my most beloved pursuits, and catapult me into the upper echelon of other talented greats.

Several weeks later while preparing a talk for our midweek service, I was deliberating over how to present a fresh and relevant explanation of effective evangelism. I got to thinking about what Christ would suggest if he were in the room with me physically. How would he avert getting stumped in a spiritual conversation? What would he say to alleviate the fear and timidity and insecurities that people face when talking about God?

I thought back to that video series—what a gift it would be if there were a training video from *our* Master on how to successfully steer people toward God! It would be so helpful to watch a scene-by-scene example of how to develop friendships, how to discover stories, and how to discern next steps—all from Jesus' perspective.

I could just imagine it. The FBI warning fades out as riveting graphics introduce the real meat of the video. Some spokesperson walks toward the camera, his sleeves rolled up and his hands hanging loosely out of his front pockets. "Plans for anything exciting today? You're sitting there on your couch with a days-old beard and pajama pants staring at a TV screen, supposing it will be another blasé Saturday afternoon. But my guess is you'd be up for a little adventure if something were to come along. What if I told you that today your predictable, routine-driven life could bump up against another person's life and change them for the better—forever?"

He stops moving on that word: *forever*. Don't we *all* want to be about something that will last forever?

My mind raced as I tried to envision the script for such a video. I needed content. Data. Facts that would support this new context for explaining how Jesus initiated conversations with strangers whose paths he crossed. Proof of what was on his mind when he found himself talking with someone about his Father. How far he would take a particular conversation, and how he would know when enough was enough.

Immediately, I began scouring the New Testament, reading and rereading his interactions with people in hopes of amassing a few lessons from the real Master regarding how to steer people toward faith in a natural, practical, and appropriate way.

One conversation stuck out.

In what I believe is the most wisdom-dense demonstration of relational intelligence, the well-worn story of Jesus' encounter with a woman beside a well became brand new for me that day. I grabbed a mug of hot coffee, felt my spine relax against the back of the desk chair, and focused complete attention on John chapter 4 as I pictured the opening scene.

TRANSFORMATION IN THE MOST UNLIKELY OF PLACES

It has been an impossibly hot day, and Jesus and his twelve disciples are seen trekking across an arid part of the Middle East, stopping partway on their journey to cool off and to get a drink of water. The sun is beginning its descent in the westward sky as dusk slowly drags in, all of the region welcoming relief from the burnt desert.

His disciples have only recently departed to buy food in town when Jesus leans forward at the waist, feeling the backs of his thighs hit the edge of the enormous well. *Ah, to sit down for a minute*, he thinks, having journeyed all day. He bows his head, closing his eyes to avoid the sun's direct contact, when a young woman approaches from the distance, evidently walking from the nearby village to draw water.

Afterward, she'll head back into town—it's a typical practice on a typical day, except for the fact that Jesus is in the mix. Taking her in as she approaches, Jesus notes that she's a Samaritan—viewed as a half-breed in those days. The well-known norms surrounding interaction with Samaritans flood his thoughts, but Jesus swats them away like pesky flies. He keeps his seat, makes eye contact with the woman, and says, "Would you please give me a drink of water?"

The woman does a double-take. Astonished, she twists her neck, looking over each shoulder as her eyes cut back to the man. *Did anyone else hear that?* She glances at Jesus, her countenance giving away her incredulity—and her displeasure. "How come you, a *Jew*, are asking me, a Samaritan woman, for water?"

As an aside, not only is there deep prejudice between the Jews and the Samaritans politically and theologically, but in those days a deep gender bias was also known to rear up its ugly head. Jewish men rarely acknowledged a woman's presence in public—let alone talked to her. Suffice it to say, a Jew shouldn't have been talking openly to a Samaritan. A man shouldn't have been talking publicly to a woman. But in the midst of the tension, Jesus ignores propriety and poses his question.

Back to the scene. "How come you, a *Jew*, are asking me, a Samaritan woman, for water?" Her tone is harsh, but Jesus doesn't flinch. Her response came in the form of a question, in Jesus' estimation an open door for further dialogue.

He notices the look of worldliness and weariness in the woman's eyes as he puts his palms beside his legs on the hot brick of the well's edge. He lifts his eyes as he stands to cross the well area. *What will this woman be able to relate to?* he wonders as he walks. *Something easy to engage in and natural to talk about, that's what I need here....*

It took him no time to land on the right topic of conversation. They are both standing at a well to retrieve one thing. And so they talk about water.

"If you knew the generosity of God and who I am, you would be asking *me* for a drink and I'd give you fresh, living water," he says.

The woman responds, "But you don't even have a bucket to draw with, and the well is very deep. How are you going to get this 'living water'?"

Jacob's well was believed to be the deepest well in the region. *Surely you don't think you're greater than our father Jacob*, she thinks. She's skittish but does a decent job of masking her concern. *Who is this weird stranger, talking about "living water"?* Her imagination kicks into overdrive. In those days, *living water* meant "running water"—but for some reason she senses a different connotation in Jesus' words.

Noticing a distinct opportunity to move from surface to spiritual things, Jesus perseveres. He knows that the material world and the spiritual world are not as far apart as this woman might believe. "Everyone who drinks this water will get thirsty again and again," he says, "but anyone who drinks the water I give will never thirst. The water I give will be an artesian spring within, gushing fountains of endless life!"

This sounds quite bizarre to the woman, all this talk of magical wells that suddenly spring up inside of people. After all, what does she know of spiritual things—of being empowered by the Spirit of God?

The woman eyes him curiously, wondering if he really means what he's saying. Self-interest surfaces as she takes the bait. "Then give me this water so that I won't get thirsty—so that I won't have to come back to this well day after day, ever again!" *I may not get all of this guy's crazy talk*, she thinks, *but if he can tell me how to avoid making this back-breaking trip every day, I'm interested!*

Jesus knows that the solution he has offered her will quench her thirst not just once, but for a lifetime. It will remove her striving not only for a season, but for all of eternity. But she can't grasp this yet. He knows his words are silliness to her—that she has no capacity for understanding the deep truths he is revealing. Looking toward the village she calls home, he shifts gears. "Go call your husband and then come back," he tells her.

The comment catches her off guard. "I don't have a husband," she responds. Which is technically true. The woman isn't currently married but does have a live-in boyfriend. Jesus, who is supernaturally equipped to know everything about everything, is all too aware of her situation.

"That's nicely put: 'I don't have a husband.' You've had *five* husbands, and the man you're living with now isn't even your husband!" His eerie insight into her life isn't lost on her. What's more, Jesus tries to affirm the fact that at least she didn't lie about her circumstances—albeit with a hint of sarcasm. He acknowledges her careful choice of words, designed to avoid the judgment and shame of admitting her involvement outside of wedlock. It's almost as if he says, "You know, you could have just lied to me outright, but you chose differently. I'll give you that."

She's staring at her feet, growing more and more uncomfortable as she wonders where the conversation is going with this unusual Jewish rabbi. Regaining her composure, she tries to divert him. "Oh, so now you're a prophet!" she laughs, rolling her eyes. "Well, if that's the case, then answer *this* one, Mr. Know-It-All. Our ancestors worshiped God at this mountain, but you Jews insist that Jerusalem is the only appropriate place for worship, right?"

Jesus indulges her question briefly but then steers things back to the issue at hand. "The time will come when it won't matter a hill of beans *where* you worship. That time is *already* here, in fact. Now that I've arrived, what matters is whether or not you believe in me for your faith—that's it. The kind of worship my father wants is not based in ritual or ceremony ... or geography. It's based only in faith. Your physical body can be anywhere on earth—on a mountaintop or in a temple ... or even beside a well on a blazing hot afternoon—and your spirit can still worship God.

"Listen, I know about your past," he continues. "But because of who I am, you still qualify for the living water I mentioned. Despite your past struggles and your present situation, this water is available for you to have, free of charge."

And as Jesus enfolds this sin-scarred woman with grace and acceptance, the icy outer layer of her heart slowly melts away. Her eyes cloud over with tears, her thirsty soul soaking up the first few drops of a good, old-fashioned rain.

* * * * •

I got up to refill my coffee cup and realized I had been sitting in the same position for the better part of an hour. That particular text from John 4 was so captivating to me because it really was a wellspring of evangelistic lessons from our Master—all gleaned from that simple, dusty patch of land in first-century Samaria.

Having the story fresh in my mind, my hope swelled regarding Christ-followers' ability to learn how to communicate the gospel appropriately and effectively. Maybe Jesus had left behind his own "Lessons from the Master" video after all. See if these ideas are as helpful to you as they were to me.

LESSON #1: BRIDGE THE CHASM

Most modern-day Christ-followers have been told since they were little kids to separate themselves from the world. They've been warned about the places they should never be caught dead in and the types of people to steer clear of—counsel that only serves to make Christians impotent, paranoid, and insular. But the first lesson Christ teaches us in this story is that we don't have to be intimidated by the differences we see in other people, whether those differences are based on race, religion, gender, or politics. Instead, we can become more like Christ, learning to model his fascination with building bridges over divides instead of deepening them.

Jesus' mission is most affirmed when wanderers come home. And while he was here on earth, he knew that the best way to lead them home is to find them where they live, relate with them as they are, and then walk by their side, stride by stride toward the Father.

In my opinion, it's the perfect description of the first *D* in 3D living—developing friendships. With those who are lovely. With those who are unlovely. With the successful and the struggling. With the outgoing and the recluse. With the accepted and the outcast. With those who are just like us and with those who are far different. I've tried to make a point of forcing myself into unnatural and uncomfortable social situations for the explicit purpose of stretching my boundaries in this regard. And what I've discovered is that people who are different from me are endlessly intriguing!

· · · · •

Recently, I had an unusual experience. I was invited by a few world leaders to participate in a think tank in downtown Manhattan. The track I was specifically invited to play a role in sought to address the tension between

Muslims and Christians. As you know, the current state of affairs there isn't pretty. Christians are getting more and more defensive. Muslims are becoming increasingly distrustful. And the rhetoric being lobbed back and forth only grows louder with each passing day.

Seated around the table with me that day were some very impressive people from the Muslim world as well as several high-powered Western leaders, three or four of whom were Christians. We spent multiple hours talking with one another about how to get along in the world. I expected the meeting to be intense, but what I didn't anticipate was how thoroughly stimulating it would be.

I came away from that experience with a better understanding of the people of Islam and refueled motivation for staying engaged in solution-seeking. I was incredibly grateful to have been part of the conversation—and more grateful still to have been stretched in such significant ways.

Think about it: Jesus could have turned his back on the woman at the well and said, "You know, I don't relate with people from other faith systems...." But thankfully, he didn't. As a result, there are a few questions we must continually ask ourselves.

- Does the Holy Spirit have my ear in situations when I'm with people from other religions or backgrounds or political persuasions?
- As I interact with people in everyday conversations, am I focused on breaking down stereotyping and building bridges instead?
- Am I actively seeking out ways to be stretched—such as sitting with someone from another generation, frequenting restaurants where the servers or owners are of a different ethnicity, or taking an interest in a culture that's different from my own?

Take big steps. Take small steps. Take whatever steps you can take in this regard so that the chasm-bridging attitude of Christ will be more fully formed in you.

LESSON #2: ASK A QUESTION

We've established that Jesus was intentional about moving toward people who were different than he was. But equally important, he was intentional about the first thing that came out of his mouth when he interacted with them. With the woman at the well, as you'll recall, it was a question. He asked a simple question to test the waters and to see if she was willing to keep talking.

. . . . •

I was in a coffee shop recently to grab some fuel before a string of afternoon meetings. I'd looked forward to stopping by because the owner was typically there, and he and I had been building rapport over several months. As I walked in and scanned the crowd, I tried to catch sight of him.

As was always the case in this particular shop, the service that day was flawless. When it was my turn in line, I ordered the usual and stepped aside, eyes still darting past the anonymous faces. I turned around to leave and saw the owner approaching me, customary smile on his face. We greeted each other as I pulled him aside to get us out of the flow of the crowd. Drawing on the experience I'd just had, I asked, "How do you train your employees to be as *good* as they are? They are always so courteous, well trained, and enthusiastic! How do you do it?"

The question was nothing profound, but his response led to an open door for further conversation. I probably could have asked him anything under the sun and he would have engaged—that's the nature of divine interactions. And who knows what types of conversations the Holy Spirit will prompt us to have in the future. Again, my role is not to determine the outcome. My role is to step out in faith, start a conversation, ask a question, explore whether there is an open door. And to leave the rest up to God.

Throughout the New Testament, if someone refused to listen to Jesus and instead closed the door, he refrained from barging through. We can learn something from this! Here's the power of Jesus' approach: asking questions allowed him to test openness in the other person's heart so that he didn't unknowingly presume some deep spiritual diatribe on them. He'd ask a thought-provoking question and then rely on the answer to tell him how quickly or slowly to move in the conversation.

First Corinthians 2:14–16 says that "the person without the Spirit [an unbeliever] does not accept the things that come from the Spirit of God but considers them foolishness, and cannot understand them because they are discerned only through the Spirit.... But we [believers] have the mind of Christ." The idea here is that people who have not yet invited Christ to come into their lives are not accustomed to spiritual conversations. And if you steamroll your way into one before establishing any relational credibility, you'll find yourself standing there with a stubbed toe (or worse yet, a black eye), wondering what just happened.

If you're uncomfortable thinking up questions to ask, just do what Jesus did. When he was beside a well, Jesus chose to ask about water. Think the woman could relate to that? She was someone who made the long walk to the well, dipped a bucket into its deep chamber to fill it with water, and then schlepped it all the way back to the village day after day after day.... Of course she could.

To fit this concept into a more recent framework, you and I both experienced something dreadfully similar during the days and months following 9/11. Interestingly, in the midst of tremendous sorrow and national upheaval, there was unprecedented openness in people's hearts and minds to spiritual things.

Many Christ-followers took the opportunity in social settings to ask people where they were on 9/11. "What did you feel once you realized what was happening?" they would ask. "Did you wonder about whether or not anyone's in charge?" And often, after asking people far from God how they dealt with their feelings following such a horrific event, God swung a door wide open to allow for spiritual, redemptive dialogue.

We can all get better at this. We can all learn how to ask people thought-provoking questions that may lead to deeper conversations. Garry Poole wrote a book several years ago entitled *The Complete Book of Questions.*[5] I highly recommend picking it up—you'll never again be caught "question-less" when a God moment unfolds right before your eyes.

Here are a few to whet your appetite:

- Why do you think there are so many religions in the world?
- Do you think it's possible for anyone to really know if there is a God?
- What do you think are the most common misconceptions people have about God?
- Do you think there's really such a thing as "unconditional love"?
- How has your belief or disbelief in God affected your life?
- Do you believe God is actively involved in our world?

- Is there such a thing as "destiny"?
- What do you hope is true about God?

You can adjust the questions I've listed to fit your surroundings and your style, or you can come up with a few original ones of your own. Doesn't matter to me; what *does* matter is that, for the sake of the kingdom, you don't rest until you become a good questioner.

LESSON #3: PRACTICE PATIENCE

Looking back on the John 4 account, have you ever stopped to wonder why Jesus was so patient with the Samaritan woman? Here's my guess: Jesus understood that he wasn't just dealing with an evangelistic project; he was dealing with a real person who had real needs. He knew that before she could begin dealing correctly with her sin issues, she had to become a believer first. Because he had his expectations set correctly, Jesus was able to treat her with dignity and encouragement instead of judgment and condemnation. As the second person of the Trinity, Jesus had access to the entire universe of information about this woman that you and I wouldn't have had. But despite his knowledge of her problem-laden past, he didn't rub her face in it. Instead, he chose to fan a *future* flame in her. "The days ahead don't have to be the same for you," he probably said.

Evidently, it was just the glimmer of hope she needed. The text says that once the woman received grace, she ran back to the village to tell all of her friends about this man who "knew everything" about her. In her haste, she left her water pot there at the well—significant because water was such a precious commodity in those days. Here she was, a sin-scarred woman who had been freshly converted. Now, more than anything else—even ensuring her water supply for the day—she desired to tell everyone how Jesus gave her a new future and a new hope. Despite countless details the Bible could have given us about the mental, spiritual, and physical state she was in when she first received grace, all we learn is that she dropped everything and ran off to tell her friends her good news. Christ's patience paid off, wouldn't you agree?

You and I have been redeemed and restored for a similar purpose—a purpose that is just as notable as spending eternity with God in heaven. You and I are expected and encouraged to share our salvation with others so that God's ultimate agenda is served—that all people would come to know him as Father.

LESSON #4: BEWARE OF RABBIT TRAILS

Here's one of my favorites: Did you notice how when things get a little tense in their conversation, the Samaritan woman tries to get Jesus off track? He's trying to stay focused on her need for God, and she starts haggling with him over which mountain people should worship on.

Happens all the time to me. I take one tiny step to point someone toward God, and instantly they bolt. Any available rabbit trail is pursued to resist having to make a decision for Christ. I call it "Spiritual ADHD." I don't know about your experience, but in my world, it seems like whenever a conversation starts heading in a spiritual direction, the most incredible questions suddenly pop up: "What about all the hypocrites who run around in Christian circles?" Or "Don't you think you're being a little exclusive? I mean, don't *all* roads lead to God?" Or "This all sounds fine, but really now, can a billion Muslims all be wrong?" Or "Hey, I hear what you're saying about God and everything, but what about those people in the tribal villages of outer Mongolia who've never heard this stuff?"

In those critical few seconds, we have to discern if the question being lobbed our way is a "left-field" question or a genuine "stumbling-block" question.

        · · · · •

I'd made great progress with a guy over the course of several weeks one time, and his interest level in spiritual things was cresting. Shortly thereafter, I felt prompted to steer him toward a decision point, and so I drew out the plan of salvation for him on a napkin. Which is when things broke down. Out of the blue, this is what he asked: "Before you go any further, Bill, what's the whole deal with creation versus evolution?"

In the space of about three seconds, I had to make a judgment call. Was this a random, left-field question, or was it really a show stopper—a stumbling-block question? Trusting that the Holy Spirit was guiding me, I said, "Listen, that's a discussion that people with a lot of letters behind their names have debated at scholarly levels for centuries. If you'd like to investigate the issue, I'd be happy to recommend a few books for you to read or for us to read together; I assure you there will be time to do that in the future. But for now, it might make sense for us to deal with how you can be made right with God...."

Guess what? The solution sounded perfectly acceptable to him. I think all he needed to know was that I was genuinely willing to indulge any sincere question he wanted to ask, as long as we didn't have to address them all in that very moment.

Sometimes, though, you will be partway through a spiritual conversation, and the person you're talking to presents an insurmountable issue that warrants immediate attention.

Once I was at a critical point in such a discussion when the other person said, "I understand most of what you're saying, but it all seems to be based on the Bible. How do we know the Bible is even real? If you're asking me to make a huge decision like this, based on a book I don't believe is true, well ... I can't."

As you'd expect, I backed myself out of the gospel presentation and chose another course of action. I had to help him address that fundamental issue before he could take even one step forward, and so we read books together, we listened to tapes together, we had further discussions on the matter, and so on. It would have been a poor decision to force his hand when he had a deal-breaking issue weighing heavily on his heart and mind.

LESSON #5: GIVE HOPE TO THE HOPELESS

Want one more? Like Christ, we should all be so bold in mentioning the astounding benefits of participating in the Christian faith. Tell people with confidence what the Father promises! To the thirsty woman Jesus encountered at the well, he offered "living" water—soul-quenching and spirit-lifting water of life. For the people you encounter, the offers are limitless:

- To those filled with shame, "Grace and forgiveness can come your way."
- To those bound up in destructive habits, "When the Son sets you free, you'll be free indeed."

- To the weak, "Strength from God — the Strength-Giver — can be yours for the asking."
- To the weary, "Jesus promises rest for your soul."
- To the poor, richness of spirit.
- To the lacking, provision in due time.
- To the grieving, consolation and comfort.
- To the sick and dying, eternal life and new bodies in the life hereafter.

One of Greg Ferguson's songs, "Peacemaker," beautifully declares some one-word benefits of staying knitted to the heart of God. Who does God promise to be in the lives of his kids? I'll let Greg's lyrics answer that:

> *Peacemaker. Fear-taker. Soul-soother. Storm-smoother.*
> *Light-shiner. Lost-finder. Cloud-lifter. Deliverer.*
> *Mind-clearer. Sigh-hearer. Hand-holder. Consoler.*
> *Wound-binder. Tear-drier. Strength-giver. Provider.*
> *Heart-healer. Kind father*
> *Peacemaker to me.*

This is the God we serve, friends.

∘ ∘ ∘ ∘ ●

When Jesus was pointing people to faith, he unapologetically told them that the life he offered was the best kind of life any human being could ever experience. In the gospel of Matthew, he compared it to a pearl of great price, which he said would be worth giving up *everything* to attain. "If you want life in all its fullness," he said, "if you want high-definition, surround-sound, heart-pounding action, there's only one place you're going to find it. A life like *that* is a life fully yielded to the God of the universe!"

I hope we'll renew our commitment to exhibiting this level of confidence and passion when talking about our faith. Is there a more important message than the one *we're* carrying to the world?

THE FOOD THAT REALLY SATISFIES

The story in John 4 takes an interesting turn once the disciples are back on the scene. To pick up where we left off, John 4:27 reveals that as the woman was tasting grace for the first time, Jesus' disciples returned and were aghast to find him hanging out with such an undignified woman. They may not have verbalized it, but their faces gave them away. Surely the *Messiah* wouldn't be mixing it up with the likes of this sinful woman! They just couldn't believe that *some* people could truly be transformed.

Oblivious to the disciples' scathing glances, the Samaritan woman rushes right past them to tell the townspeople of her magnificent interaction with a certain Rabbi she'd met. With her now out of the picture, the disciples try to get Jesus to eat some lunch. They'd eaten in town and knew he was probably famished from baking in the hot sun for hours after what had already been an exhausting trip from Judea.

It's obvious his young apprentices have no clue about all that had unfolded while they were gone. "Don't you see? I've just had a fantastic meal," he said. The disciples looked at each other, confusion racing across their faces. *What in the world is he talking about? Did he scrounge food from someone while we were gone?*

But Jesus wasn't referring to meat-and-potatoes food; he was talking about *soul* food. And this type of food was as good as it got for him! While his men were in town munching on a few greasy olives and a couple of stale loaves of bread, Christ had just enjoyed the equivalent of a seven-course meal!

The end result of Jesus' "meal" was unbelievable. We later learn that the Samaritan woman returned to the scene after grabbing half the townspeople and dragging them back to the well to see Jesus. The next thing you know, they listened to Jesus teach, and many crossed the line of faith right there on the spot. All because of one man who seized a God-given opportunity to offer hope to a woman desperately in need of it.

"Look around you!" Jesus must have rebuked the disciples as that day came to a close. "How much riper do you think these Samaritan fields are going to get! Don't you agree that these people need to be rescued from their selfishness and false religion? Guys, it's harvesttime! If you are patient and commit to persevering with *that* woman's level of zeal for lost souls, you'll reap more fruit than you've ever seen."

·   ·   ·   ·   •

When I mulled over the text that afternoon in my study, I was amazed once again by how quickly the Samaritan woman shifted from hostile to respectful, obstinate to pliable, self-centered to Christlike. And all in a matter of four verses. God only knows when salvation is right around the corner for someone. Our job is to stay the course, walking when we are prompted to walk, talking when we are prompted to talk, staying quiet when silence is required, and trusting God with the outcome of redeeming his broken and sin-scarred people.

STEPS THAT CHANGE THE WORLD

Think of it: because of one woman's transformation, countless other lives were transformed. Can't you just imagine her life fifteen or twenty years later? I envision her entire family gathered together, the kids and grandkids enjoying Christian fellowship and the mercies of God. The entire family is relaxing together, telling stories about their lives, their lineage, their longings. One of the grandkids pipes up from across the room and says, "Where did all of this start, anyway? You know, our faith."

The Samaritan woman who had been redeemed pipes up from across the room, granddaughter on her lap as she rocks back and forth. "Children, it all started beside a well—Jacob's well, in fact. Our faith heritage traces back to a dusty well area where Jesus Christ himself—the Messiah in the flesh—left a Circle of Comfort and walked across the sand to approach your soiled-souled grandmother.

"Jesus took those first few steps to reach out to me, extending a hand of love and compassion in a day when nobody else would. And now, because he has cared so deeply for us, children, we will care for others—especially those who don't yet know him."

· · · · •

Think about your own story for a moment. How did you wind up in the kingdom of God? As I've ruminated on this, I have begun challenging people to pay close attention to that question. In terms of the walk-across-the-room metaphor, I believe ten out of ten people would agree that when they boil down their salvation experience, it always involved one person making a decision to walk toward them and reach out a hand of friendship. Someone taking a risk for them to bridge an ethnic, religious, or socioeconomic chasm. Someone investing time to wonder about their eternal destiny. Someone exerting a little effort to interest them in the possibility that they could know the love of God and be freed from their sin someday.

As the Samaritan woman experienced, the same care and compassion that drew you into the kingdom is yours to extend to someone else now. You can get better at avoiding embarrassing mistakes when sharing your faith. You can get better at confidently explaining the crux of God's redemptive story. You can get better at engaging with people as magnificent creations instead of as projects.

The powerful, redemptive story of the woman at the well is much more than just a good example of living in 3D. And Christ is more than a mere subject-matter expert who's willing to toss out a few success tips on evangelism. Friends, he is our constant companion, living inside of us to prompt us toward Christlikeness, and working through us to point others toward faith.

God says that if you are a follower of Christ, he has poured pure water over you and has scrubbed you clean. He has given you a new heart, replacing the stone one with a heart that's God-willed, not self-willed. He has put his Spirit in you and makes it possible for you to do what he asks you to do so that you can live every day in freedom. The living water that he offered to the woman at the well so many years ago is now bubbling and coursing and rushing right inside of your heart.

And it's there for a reason! It exists not only that your eternal thirst might be quenched, but also that you would walk into work each day choosing to be focused on more than just the "business at hand." That you would be tender toward the Spirit's prompt to cross an office complex or a construction site or a school building. That you would remember Christ's blood, shed for each and every person you see. That you would put some action behind your faith as you cross a room, look a person directly in the eyes, and ask, "Would you like a cup of water?"

STUDY QUESTIONS

1. Like the woman at the well, have you ever felt dusty, weary, and worn down by life? What experience comes to mind?

2. Jesus' response to the woman at the well was acceptance rather than condemnation and forgiveness rather than rebuke. How have you experienced God's acceptance and forgiveness in your own life?

3. One of the lessons from this chapter is that as Christ-followers, we should be in the business of bridging chasms. On page 156 you read that it's important to develop friendships with "those who are lovely. With those who are unlovely. With the successful and the struggling. With the outgoing and the recluse. With the accepted and the outcast. With those who are just like us and with those who are far different." As you assess your own friendship patterns, whom do you typically reach out to?

   ☐ Lovely people   OR ☐ People who are difficult to love

   ☐ Successful people   OR ☐ People who are struggling

   ☐ Those who are outgoing   OR ☐ Recluses

   ☐ People who are easy to accept OR ☐ Those who are outcasts

   ☐ People who are just like you   OR ☐ People far different from you

   Why do you think Christ encourages his followers to be radically accepting of *all* people?

4. Greg Ferguson's song "Peacemaker" articulates many of God's promises to his children. Which of the following roles do you most need God to play in your life today and why?

   ☐ Peacemaker   ☐ Fear-taker   ☐ Soul-soother

   ☐ Storm-smoother   ☐ Light-shiner   ☐ Lost-finder

   ☐ Cloud-lifter   ☐ Deliverer   ☐ Mind-clearer

   ☐ Sigh-hearer   ☐ Hand-holder   ☐ Consoler

   ☐ Wound-binder   ☐ Tear-drier   ☐ Strength-giver

   ☐ Provider   ☐ Heart-healer   ☐ Kind Father

5. Are there people in your world who might also need to know that God can soothe their souls, smooth their storms, and dry their tears? Ask God supernaturally to reveal the needs of people in your life, and then find a way—whether by phone or email or a letter or an in-person visit—to tell them with confidence that there is a God in heaven who created them, who loves them, who has already gone before them, and who will be their everlasting Peacemaker if they so choose.

PART IV

Grander Vision Living

CHAPTER 9

Big-Fish Invitations

During his three-year teaching ministry, Jesus had a rather interesting habit. He'd walk around, see people who needed assistance, and then go so far as to suspend the natural laws that govern the universe in order to help them. Suddenly, the diseased would be healed, the blind would see, the deaf would hear, the mute would sing, and the paralyzed would get up and dance. All because Jesus Christ took action.

According to recorded history, it happened at least forty times, and as you might expect, this type of odd behavior was met with a mixed response. While some people were delighted by his displays of power, most people in first-century Palestine had no idea what to make of a guy whose life was marked by such peculiarity.

In my estimation, taking into account the dozens of miracles he performed, there's one that stands out as being the *oddest*. You probably remember the event. It involved him providing not healing or hearing or sight, but rather an enormous catch of fish to a couple of frustrated fishermen one day.

Luke 5 says that Simon Peter and his brother Andrew were washing their nets on the shore of the Sea of Galilee after a long, futile night at sea. It would otherwise have been a picture-perfect day beside the stunning blue waters of the narrow inland lake. But since the fish hadn't cooperated with the "big catch" plan the night before, the task of picking seaweed out of nets proved utterly defeating.

As they diligently worked, they caught sight of Jesus, who was teaching a group of listeners farther up the shoreline. Evidently, the audience liked what he had to say, because the longer he taught, the more the crowd swelled. (Interesting how my teaching typically has the opposite effect. . . .)

Eventually, the group surrounding Jesus grew to be so large that he had to find a way to get some distance from them so he could be seen and heard amid the chaos. He quickly landed on a solution. If he could row out a few feet from shore in a boat, he figured, then he could keep on preaching from the floating pulpit. And apparently, out of all of the boats lining the shore, Jesus chose Peter's. Without any word of explanation, he hopped on board, asked Peter to jump in and row him out a little ways, and then continued to teach.

Once he'd finished his talk, most of the crowd dispersed as Jesus sat down in the boat to chat with Peter. At some point in their conversation, Jesus made an interesting request of his captive audience. "Put out into deep water, and let down the nets for a catch," he said.[6] *Let's see if we can't have a little fun here*, Jesus probably thought.

Peter was skeptical, to say the least. He and his partners had already been fishing all night—to no avail. Maybe it's just me, but as I read the text, I imagine Peter becoming a bit put out by Jesus, who'd evidently been sleeping while Peter and the other guys were slaving away at sea. And now Jesus, by Peter's standards a guy who was a little lacking in fishing expertise, had the audacity to instruct *Peter*, a career fisherman, on how to catch fish? You'd have probably copped a little attitude too if you were in his sandals.

But his better judgment kicks in as he disguises his doubt and obliges Jesus' request. The nets get tossed over the side of the boat, and the catch that results from his obedience is so huge that he has to call in reinforcements. "Guys, you're not gonna believe this!" he must have hollered to his stunned buddies who were standing on shore. "But I've got a boatload of fish here . . . literally! Could you get out here to help lug in these fish? And *pronto*?!"

James and John launch their boat and start rowing for all they're worth to help out their partner. The three fishermen muscle the bulging nets back into the boats, the hoards of brown and silver fish teeming with energy. As they arrive back on shore, I picture the remnant of the crowd that hung around to see what all the commotion was about applauding and cheering the fishermen's monstrous effort.

Elated by the turn of events, Peter, James, and John jump around, whooping and hollering as they celebrate the mother lode of all fishing. Jesus looks on, thinking that the passion, the energy of these young men is unlike anything he's ever seen. He knows there's something special about these three, and so he entices them with a few moments of vision-casting in hopes of staying in their worlds a little while longer.

DOLLARS VERSUS DESTINIES

I imagine Jesus laughing as he tries unsuccessfully to get the guys' attention in the midst of their exuberance. "Hey, guys! You think *that* was something? You think netting a bunch of scaly underwater creatures was fun? Try thinking a *grander* thought for a second.... Listen, how about multiplying the fun-factor you experienced in the last few minutes by about a thousand!

"Not that there's anything wrong with catching fish. I know you're trying to earn a living, and taking fish to market day in and day out to earn a few dollars is as good a way as any. But instead of netting a few dollars, just imagine landing a few *destinies*.

"*That's* where the action is!"

Jesus' eyes probably glistened with enthusiasm at this point, the men's rapt attention spurring him on. "Peter, James, John," Jesus said as he looked each of them in the eyes, "so far, you three have spent your days being fishermen. But what I'm inviting you to do—starting right here, right now—is to become fishers of *men and women*. Instead of investing your precious time and energy in catching six-inch fish, let's go after the six-footers! I'm asking you to give up everything you have and everything you are for the sake of people's souls. Come with me, and you'll see what *real* living is all about!"

*　　*　　*　　*　　•

Now, let me push pause on the scene for a second. Wouldn't you agree that supernaturally filling some fishing nets is a fairly odd means of recruiting a few disciples? It certainly seems strange to me, but here's what gets me most about this miracle: I believe it sets up one of the most critical aspects of Jesus' teaching, this idea of small fish versus big fish. Because from the moment he arrived on the scene until today, Jesus has been asking all sorts of people — fishermen and businessmen and housewives and teachers and preachers and lawyers and all the rest — this one question: *Are you going to throw your one and only life into pursuing small fish, or will you risk tossing your nets out there in anticipation of catching the human-sized ones?*

And you've got to love Jesus' perfect timing in getting his point across. He waited until these three hard workers had experienced some measure of success — the catch probably represented their best business day to date — and then he pulled them aside and tried the "Emeril approach" on them. I'm sure Jesus nailed the Cajun accent as he said, "Hey, netting some perch is fine. But now let's kick it up a notch!" And the guys who would be his first three disciples accepted his invitation right there on the spot.

"Fishers of men and women?" they must have wondered out loud.

"Yeah. Yeah, I can just see it!" Peter chimed in. "No more small fish for us.... Starting today, we're going after the big ones!"

THE ONLY LIFE HE KNEW

Peter probably expected to earn his living as a fisherman for the rest of his days. His home was at sea. Motion. Wind. Waves. Saltwater. Netting the next catch. These things were all he knew.

But the picture of the future that Jesus painted that afternoon stirred something deep inside him. It set him off in a new direction, and the contrast made his day-to-day existence instantly mundane.

How compelling was Jesus' invitation? The various gospel accounts imply that Peter's decision to follow Christ meant forsaking his livelihood, his routine, and even his family. As Jesus carefully exposed Peter and his impressionable friends to the big-fish opportunity, he set their hair on fire for the only mission in life that is worth pursuing — the mission of finding those who are lost, serving those who are under-resourced, and loving those who have been forgotten. It's what I call "Grander Vision Living."

And in my opinion, Jesus has never stopped jumping into the boats of people who might be willing to sell out to the Grander Vision. If you want a compelling example of what this looks like in modern times, let's take a closer look at my friend Chuck Colson's before-and-after story.

.   .   .   .   •

Chuck Colson served as chief counsel to President Nixon from 1969 until 1973. For years, he operated in the epicenter of political, social, and economic power and privilege. By all accounts, Chuck was living the good life. Here was a guy who knew all the right people and was constantly surrounded by the country's elite. But things aren't always what they appear to be.

Although Colson wasn't directly involved in the infamous Watergate scandal that ultimately led to Nixon's resignation, some peripheral activities would land him in an Alabama prison for seven months. He would find himself plummeting from the pinnacle to the depth of life, all in the blink of an eye. From the penthouse to the outhouse, as my sailing friends would say.

But another turn of events would unexpectedly unfold first.

To fully appreciate Colson's transformation, you have to understand how desperately he searched for significance in everything *except* in a relationship with Jesus Christ—he looked to his college education. His academic honors. His military recognition. His law degree. Even his experience working beside the president of the United States (a role that began when Chuck was only thirty-nine). But at the end of the day, he still felt empty, hollow, purposeless, and defeated. None of his pursuits had scratched his soul's itch.

After several conversations with a businessman friend—as well as a powerful encounter with C. S. Lewis's *Mere Christianity*—Colson submitted his life to Christ. It was the first step toward a future that would far surpass even Chuck's highly notable past. And once the Grander Vision had seized him, he committed the rest of his life to helping people get back on their feet after serving time in prison. But more important, he devoted himself to helping free people from the darkest prison of all—the prison of the soul—by introducing them to things like purpose, inclusion, and hope.

In his book *How Now Shall We Live?* Colson reflects on more than two decades spent helping former inmates reach their God-given potential. He recounts one inspiring journey he made to the Philippines, where dark, deplorable conditions existed all around him.

*   *   *   *   ●

As the story goes, an entrepreneurially minded inmate of the Mantalupa Prison had been led to Christ through Colson's worldwide organization, Prison

Fellowship International (PFI). After he had been mentored, coached, and developed by several of PFI's staff members, the former convict devised a simple plan to aid his fellow inmates.

Through the aid of local churches, recently released prisoners would receive a $120 advance to use in purchasing a pedicab—a bicycle equipped with a built-in sidecar. The vehicle was the Philippines' long-standing form of public transportation and showed up all over the streets of downtown Manila. Moreover, each of them received an introduction to the God who created them and who wanted to offer them a future that didn't resemble their past.

Over time, the former prisoners would repay their loans, and the refilled kitty would serve as a means of providing fresh batches of ex-cons with loans, for many the conduit to their first real job.

On the day that Chuck entered the grounds of PFI's headquarters in Manila, he was surprised to find thirty-five shiny pedicabs lined up in the parking lot, their bright-eyed owners and their families proudly standing beside them.

The inmates probably all shared a similar thought: *Nobody would believe the roller coaster I've been on!* They'd once been sequestered in eight-by-eight cells with no freedom to speak of, little contact with the outside world, and hardly a glimmer of anything positive in their future. Now they had independence, gainful employment, and the return of some self-respect.

As Chuck studied the humble faces he saw all along the line of re-invented men, a four-year-old girl standing about a hundred feet away from the group caught his eye. His heart melted as he watched her—as if in slow motion—run up to her father and unabashedly wrap her arms around his leg. Her father had been a prison inmate but now had a steady job, reliable income, and, most important, an air of security that comes only from Christ's enfoldment.

Her big brown eyes cut skyward toward her dad as if to say, "Daddy, I'm so glad you're home with us again!" The father stood there, his chest now puffed out some, stroking his precious daughter's hair, gently caressing her face, choking back the tears from his eyes. Later, Chuck disclosed that the joy that accompanied seeing the transformation of one man's life rose head and shoulders above every other accomplishment he had known. That powerful picture, just a momentary snapshot, made the entire quarter-life experience worthwhile.

THE PEOPLE PRIORITY

Chuck has a God-given aptitude to accept the unacceptable and to believe endlessly in the unbelievable. It's a good model for everyone who follows Christ, this ability to see people as God sees them. Time and again, when staring into the eyes of a convicted inmate, Chuck instead saw a rounded-out, fulfilled, productive life that could be used for eternal good. And with that compelling picture in mind, he threw aside everything else that vied for his attention and said yes to God's invitation to live the Grander Vision.

Chuck learned that saying yes to God's Grander Vision invitation means saying yes to people. Jesus' convictions about accepting people with the heart of the Father were so firm that when he saw someone putting a higher value on anything other than people, he would step in and say, "If you knew my Father at all, you would never allow anything to trump the value of people."

This goes back to the incurably relational aspect of God that we looked at in the chapter on developing friendships. God *loves* people! And is there any better picture of the Father's posture toward people than the open arms of Christ? Jesus told his disciples in John 14:9–10 that if they really knew him, then they would know his Father as well. "From now on," he said, "you do know my Father and have seen him. Don't you believe that I am in the Father, and that the Father is in me? The words I say to you are not just my own. Rather, it is the Father, living in me, who is doing his work!" The idea is that everything Jesus Christ did was dictated by his Father's inclinations, his Father's desires.

Christ's followers who choose to live the Grander Vision walk through their days with sixth-sense awareness of people—*all* people, regardless of where they are spiritually when they find them. Grander Vision Living adherents possess a supernatural ability to get past what our human senses pick up on and focus instead on the fact that every single person they meet is a child of God—and is worthy of being redeemed.

. . . . .

The book of Luke records an occasion when Jesus, James, and John were refused passage through a corner of Samaria while en route to Jerusalem. As ethnic pride welled up in the hearts of his two disciples, they asked Jesus if he wanted them to call down fire from heaven to destroy the offenders. "Let's show them who *really* has the power!" they probably threatened. But Jesus simply shook his head, realizing they didn't fully grasp the heart of the Father—the one who would have placed a higher value on the redemption of the Samaritans than on patching up the wounded pride of a couple of Jews.

At another time, a group of Pharisees caught Jesus interacting and fellowshipping with a crowd of irreligious people. "Why would you waste your time on these hell-bound pagans?" the Pharisees complained. Thinking Jesus had attached an inordinate amount of value to unworthy heathens, they were probably stung by Christ's reply. "With all of your book smarts, all of your theological degrees and your prized, law-abiding perfection, you still don't get the heart of the Father."

What was Jesus saying? That reflecting the heart of the Father always means leaning toward people—even lost people. (*Especially* lost people, as we all once were.) Why? Because he knew that the door to the kingdom is open to everyone. To people the world over, Jesus says, "Access is granted! You are welcome here in our little fellowship. Come on in and join us. Love and acceptance and grace await."

Friends, *this* is the profound message we get to carry to people who are standing on the other side of the room.

WHAT'S MOST VALUABLE?

I am deeply moved each time I read the gospel accounts that show Jesus accepting, including, and deeply loving people. Wherever he went, whomever he met—despite age, race, gender, social standing, and moral failings—Jesus always exhibited that "radical inclusiveness," as we looked at in chapter 3 on developing friendships. "Come as you are!" he would say time and time again. "The door to the kingdom is open to you ... yes, even you!"

Oh, if only my arms could be as wide open as his! If only I enfolded people with the care and compassion that he exhibited. Just imagine what would happen in our churches if every real estate broker, carpenter, airline pilot, lawyer, homemaker, businessperson among us said, "I love my job because I'm in the people business. Yeah, my pay stub is from XYZ Corporation, but my *mission* is from Christ. Because of that, I try to show Christ's care for people by throwing open my arms to the lost and the found. To the black and the white. To the rich and the poor. To the young and the old, all the while asking the Holy Spirit what he wants me to say and what he wants me to do."

Think about how far God was willing to go to prove the point that there is nothing more valuable than people. On what would be the most dreadful day of Jesus' life, God's desire to accept broken people soared so high that he allowed his only Son to suffer and die on their behalf. During wearying hours when Jesus was to face unbelievable emotional turmoil and unthinkable physical torture as he paid for the sins of the world—both yours and mine—he demonstrated once and for all that accepting sin-scarred people is of ultimate worth in life. When the executioners stripped the clothes off of his back and pounded his hands and feet to a wooden cross with barbaric nonchalance, all Jesus could do was cry, "Father, forgive them, for they do not know what they are doing."[7]

On a human level, we can't even begin to relate to his selfless compassion and endless mercy. Where was Jesus' concern for his own well-being? Where were his protests about his unsavory and painful circumstances? Where was his seething anger toward these animalistic men who were murdering him? Where was the striving for revenge?

Jesus knew the heart of the Father so intimately that even when facing death he could not let go of his preoccupation with people. As he inhaled his last breath, his heart still beat for people. As his earthly ministry came to a close, he remained clear about his mission to serve people. And as he hung there on that cross, I wonder if what flashed through his mind were the faces of the people whose lives would be forever changed because he accomplished what he came into the world to accomplish.

In his life *and* in his death, Jesus deftly and ruthlessly protected his people-priority. His every word and every action proclaimed, *There is nothing better than pouring your life into the goal of welcoming home a wandering soul!* In fact, in Luke 15:10 Jesus said in essence, "All the courts of heaven erupt in cosmic celebration when a single, sin-infested human being bends the knee in repentance and faith!" The Father's heart explodes in joy, Jesus said, over every human reclamation. Every single one!

Think about this for a minute. Do you believe this about your own process of redemption? The day you chose to submit your life to the God of the universe who created you, the entire population of heaven rose to their feet in joyous, thundering applause. Just imagine what life would be like if you lived with this same exuberance for reclaiming God's people for him!

* * * * •

I remember the season of life when our two kids were little. Lynne and I would hire a babysitter to come over so we could enjoy a night out, just the two of us. Each time, I'd pull the babysitter off to the side and remind her that the house, the car, the material things, could all disappear while we were away, but if anything happened to those two kids, well ... she wouldn't want to know what would happen. With a straight face, I'd look into the eyes of a quivering teenager and say, "Don't screw up where our kids are concerned."

And I was serious. Shauna and Todd meant the world to Lynne and me. Still do. And I expected the babysitter to treat them with equal carefulness and tenderness while they were in her care.

Friends, do you realize that humanly speaking, this is *exactly* how God feels about his kids?

Lost kids. Found kids. Young kids. Old kids. Struggling kids. Thriving kids. Lonely kids. Popular kids. He wants them all enfolded in community and care. And when Christ-followers get committed to living the Grander Vision, they automatically begin caring for God's most prized possession—his people.

This was the heart of the invitation to Peter, James, and John on that warm afternoon beside the Sea of Galilee. It's the same invitation he still extends to his followers of all shapes and sizes today. "You can get in on this too!" he promises. "You can be part of my plan to get all my kids under my umbrella of love and grace. Just imagine it! Imagine *your* life being used to help someone live abundantly today and land in heaven tomorrow. Maybe you've been fishing for paltry perch your entire life, but beginning today, you can switch gears. You can head toward helping me land the biggest fish of all … a person's *soul*."

The reality of Grander Vision Living is this: once you net a few big fish, the search for perch loses its luster. When I abandoned my business-centered career plans for a life wrapped up in full-time ministry, I never looked back. Still today, there's no way I could manufacture the same level of enthusiasm for a world that revolves solely around P&Ls and growth strategies. Because for more than thirty years now, I've been pursuing the Grander Vision. Any other endeavor would require my settling for a lesser vision.

You've already been introduced to my friend Greg Ferguson. He and I run together almost every afternoon, a habit that began in the early stages of our friendship. But what you may not know is that at the outset, Greg was a jingle writer for advertising firms in downtown Chicago. Shortly after Greg became a Christian, I began begging him to refocus some things. "Write songs that help people go to heaven," I would say. "Sing songs that will help people wind up in the right place for eternity."

Thank God, Greg crossed that line and is giving himself day by day to catalyzing people's decisions to cross the line of faith themselves. Increasingly, his life is about giving people a glimpse of the heaven that awaits them, if they so choose. And he serves as a terrific example of someone who uses his gifts, his yearnings, his abilities, to get more people into the kingdom.

Choosing the Grander Vision will look different depending on your unique set of circumstances. And just as Jesus never condemned Peter's fishing occupation, neither do I have anything against whatever pursuit you might be involved in (assuming it's legal). But also like Jesus, I intend to call you to a higher level. "Take what you're already good at … in this case, fishing," Jesus said to the fishermen, "but shift your motivation to things that are eternal. Give *every* aspect of your life to the Grander Vision! *This* is the life I came to bring you."

HITTING CLOSE TO HOME

I've been an incurable sailing fanatic for most of my life and have been blessed in the last decade or so to race in regattas all over the world. The format for most of them involves racing seven times in the span of three days. And for each individual race—known as the "dailies"—the top three finishers are awarded prizes, such as a sailing shirt or a hat with the regatta name embroidered on it.

So winning the dailies is fine, but what everybody *really* wants to take is the overall victory—the cumulative result of all seven races over the three days. Winners take home huge silver or gold platters or trophies with plaques that have their names and the regatta information engraved on them. They retain bragging rights for years to come as people admire the tall statues symbolizing real sailing success. But most important, winners of that particular regatta know deep down inside that they landed the biggest, most valuable prize available.

Suffice it to say, to a sailor worth his or her salt, the difference between winning a few dailies and taking the overall victory is profound.

One year, my team was in contention to win the overall title in the Harbor Springs Regatta on Lake Michigan. All we had to do in order to snag a trophy-yielding victory was to stay ahead of *one* competitor. It didn't matter where we finished in the lineup for that individual race, as long as we beat that one boat.

During the final leg, I saw an unbelievable opportunity to win the daily, but it would come at the risk of the overall standings. The professional tactician on board listened carefully to my thorough assessment before responding. After I finished, he looked at me and said, "Well, Bill, we could certainly do what you're suggesting. But I just have one question: Do you want the hat, or do you want the hardware?"

Needless to say, we opted for maintaining our overall standing and all ended up taking home a huge piece of silver hardware.

But my crew member's question was a good one, and it has stuck with me ever since that race. In the regatta called Life, do I want the hat or the hardware? The small fish or the big fish? The lesser vision or the grander, eternally significant one?

Let me hit a little closer to home with this concept. Recently, I received a five-page letter from an area waitress who is part of Willow Creek. Before becoming a Christian, I learned, she waited tables at a restaurant where many of us would eat after weekend services—and where Christians from other churches would hang out as well.

"Please let me convey a few things about Christians from a non-Christian waiter's perspective," her letter began. "It's quite well-known among waitstaff that when tables of Christians get seated in your section, it will be anything *but* a positive experience. Christians are demanding. They tend to stay at tables for a long time. They often try to push literature. And they rarely tip generously." (Any Lesser-Vision-Living bells ringing in your head?)

Her letter continued as my mind trailed off, dismayed over the indictment. She explained that the waitresses she worked with had finally landed on a rotation schedule so that a particular server wouldn't always get "stuck with the Christians." Five pages later, I reminded myself that this letter was penned by a woman right inside of our community. *What does this say about Christ-followers when we neglect something as basic as treating a server with kindness, respect, and gratitude?* I wondered.

How easily we forget that every person we come across is a person God loves. A person God has put in our path for us to be respectful toward. Someone to find pleasure in! Someone for *us* to serve by behaving with a Grander Vision Living attitude: "If you are scrambling and don't have time to refill my coffee cup just yet, don't worry about it. I can wait. I would be happy to wait, in fact." *This* should be our attitude, because last time I checked, we have the Holy Spirit living inside of us.

Right?

To get painstakingly practical for a moment, if you are at a restaurant and your server has seen you with your Bible open on your dining table or has heard you talking about spiritual things to the group you're eating with, please do us all a favor and remember the Grander Vision. Make sure your attitude points to the fact that Christians are supposed to be marked by love.

*   *   *   *   *

Something inside of me hesitates to use this example from my own experience because I can be such an atrocious reflection of Christ in so many situations. But here is one area where I have had some degree of consistency: on most Mondays when I need to start reading for the following week's sermon, I head to my favorite diner near the Chicago suburb of Barrington to take up residence for the better part of two hours, working through my notes at a little table in the back.

On some occasions, I will order a four-dollar breakfast, just as a frame of reference, and will leave a five-dollar tip. Now, I'm Dutch, remember, so parting with that five bucks is an emotionally charged experience for me. But here is what runs through my mind as I leave the money on the table: *Although there's really nobody else to wait on, I've still taken up one of her tables for the better part of ninety minutes with an open Bible in front of me. My waitress—often a single mom trying to make ends meet—knows good and well what I am working on.*

She knows I am working on something that has to do with God and with Christianity. My tip is going to serve as a direct reflection in her mind of how all Christians behave. And a generous tip with a sincere smile might go a long way in solidifying in her mind—at least for today—that Christ-followers really do treat others with love and kindness and respect.

I have a phrase that I communicate to servers on a frequent basis: "You have served me well." And when I find myself in the same restaurant consistently, after I tell them again and again that they have served me well, I typically add, "And if there is a way I can serve you, please let me know."

Grander Vision Living. It doesn't take much, really. Just an intentional shift in focus. From my needs and wants to those of others. From my agenda to the Spirit's prompting. From myopic Lesser Vision Living to the stimulating, abundant life that Christ came and died for.

* * * * •

I like what Romans 8 has to say about living the Grander Vision:

> *This resurrection life you received from God is not a timid, grave-tending life. It's adventurously expectant, greeting God with a childlike "What's next, Papa?" God's Spirit touches our spirits and confirms who we really are. We know who he is, and we know who we are: Father and children. And we know we are going to get what's coming to us—an unbelievable inheritance! ... The created world itself can hardly wait for what's coming next. Everything in creation is being more or less held back. God reins it in until both creation and all the creatures are ready and can be released at the same moment into the glorious times ahead. Meanwhile, the joyful anticipation deepens.*[8]

In the midst of living in an imperfect world, Romans brings us a necessary dose of encouragement: we can actually be enlarged in our waiting for the perfection of heaven. How? By choosing Grander Vision Living, asking with bated breath, "What's next, God? What do you have for me to do? Whom can I radically accept today as I wait in joyful anticipation for all that's to come?"

URGENCY REGARDING ETERNITY

The longer each of us walks with Christ, the more urgency we feel regarding eternal realities. As we become more and more transformed into his image, our ability to reflect his calculated sense of urgency regarding men and women deepens. Why? Because time is short. And although, for the Christ-follower, eternal reality equates to "glorious times ahead" as Romans says, there is unfortunately another side to the coin.

Nearly three years ago, the father of one of my friends was diagnosed with terminal colon cancer and was almost immediately given the devastating news that he had only six months left to live. My friend's dad and I had developed a strong friendship over the years, and in the spirit of trying to serve as a Resource Provider, I had sent countless books, tapes, and other things to him in an attempt to point him toward God.

But he was a self-made, self-reliant type. I knew his knee would never bend before Christ without a bitter battle for his own pride ensuing first. Soon after we learned of his prognosis, I began to visit him in the hospital as much as my schedule would allow. Each time I left his room after talking with him, my mind clicked through old memory verses that seemed to take on new meaning in light of seeing my friend lie there dying.

"Just as people are destined to die once, and after that to face judgment ..."; "Salvation is found in no one else, for there is no other name given under heaven by which we must be saved"; "For the wages of sin is death, but the gift of God is eternal life in Christ Jesus our Lord."[9]

The words washed over me with their usual hope-eliciting capability. But intermingled there was an unexpected sense of despair. I couldn't bear to know that this man would spend eternity apart from God ... and at some point, apart from me.

What I can only describe as a *captivating* sense of urgency regarding his destiny arose in my spirit. I began sending him edifying notes, dropping off more tapes and videos, and praying with increased fervency for him to submit his life to Christ. One Friday morning, in the middle of a typical work routine, I was overwhelmed by the awareness of what was hanging in the balance regarding his eternity. Dropping everything— meetings, studying, scheduling—I rushed to the hospital and stood by his bedside.

The conversation that ensued proved to be the greatest evangelistic risk I had ever taken to that point in my Christian life.

To my surprise, within moments my nerves seemed to relax as my shakiness settled into confidence. For what felt like the hundredth time, I patiently began to explain the gospel to him. *Please, God, by your Spirit ... please let this sink in.* Later that afternoon, with unabashed pleading, I asked him to open his heart to Christ and to receive the gift of eternal life. I couldn't have contrived the sincerity that I felt that day as I explained that he really could take Christ at his word, that his broken body really would be restored one day, and that his wounded soul really was headed toward healing. "Don't let another moment pass," I begged, "without being absolutely certain of your eternal destiny."

Just before noon that day, to my astonishment, he earnestly and decisively prayed to receive Christ. Twenty-two hours later, he was gone.

I officiated his memorial service the following Tuesday, and as I walked away from the grave site with friends and family, I felt sobered by the turn of events in his life. *God, please help me live every day with an awareness of eternal realities,* I thought. *Don't let me lose this Spirit-directed kind of urgency regarding your most prized possession—people!*

WHAT'S IT GOING TO BE?

I was sitting in a meeting one time when the speaker suddenly unfurled a roll of stickers in his hand. "There is something we must all understand," he said as he walked across the front of the room. Periodically, he would stop and put a red sticker on a tiny replica of a house, and a red sticker on a Hot Wheels car, and a red sticker on a dollhouse-sized desk that represented our vocational lives.

"You may not be able to tell from where you're sitting, but each red sticker has a single word on it," he said. "The word is 'temporary.' And these things I'm putting them on are all temporary. They will fade away, turning cartwheels like leaves in the wind when this world ends.

"If you are living for these things, then you are living a life of temporary pleasure, temporary satisfaction, and temporary fulfillment." He continued walking around the room, now silent as he labeled everything in sight with red stickers. I watched his hands declare the fate of the best this world has to offer as those stickers made their way to the goods in front of us.

Temporary. Temporary. Temporary. Temporary. Temporary. Temporary. Temporary.

"There is only *one* thing in this room that is not temporary," he continued. "There is only one thing that you can take with you into the next world."

He called someone up to join him on the stage, and he placed a blue sticker on her lapel. "When you get to the end of your life and take in your last breath," he said, "what do you want your life to have been about?" My heart stilled as one thought stemmed all others in my mind.

It really is all about people.

No earthly commodity is going to make it from this world into the next. Not land, not homes, not bank accounts, not titles, not achievements. Only *souls*. Friends, Jesus Christ taught that every human being would be resurrected to spend an eternity in community with God in heaven or in isolation from God in hell. And because Jesus understood these eternal realities and believed them to the core of his being, he focused his attention on the only entity that would extend into the next reality: people.

I don't know what the final assessment on my earthly life will be once I am gone. But I know this much: my quest while I am here is to seek people out and point them toward faith in God. I've tried enough approaches in my five decades of living to know that to invest yourself in anything other than people is to settle for the pursuit of a Lesser Vision — that ugly, ensnaring trap of the temporal.

If you're over the quota for Lesser Vision Living and are ready to jump into the *real* adventure, then get all over the task of refocusing your gifts and talents, your abilities and passions, toward God-ward pursuits.

The question is not whether or not you have a contribution to make. Every single one of you has an astoundingly large contribution to make. The real issue is whether or not you're investing yourself in activities that spur people toward heaven. The issue is whether or not you are leveraging your creative energies, marketing skills, and problem-solving capabilities for the sake of landing more people in heaven. The issue is whether or not you prize people enough to share the good news with them in creative and alluring ways.

·   ·   ·   ·   •

There really are a heaven and a hell. They really are eternal places—destinations of real people living real lives just next door, just across the street, just two offices down, just across the locker room. Real people who need your salt and your light in their lives. And I have to wonder, will you be the one to reach them? Will you be the one present in a church service someday when your once-wayward buddy finally stands in a baptism tank, sopping wet and ready to walk in newness of life? I guarantee that in that moment, most likely through tears, you will realize just as Chuck Colson did that you will never find significance apart from walking in God's Grander Vision.

The Grander Vision or the Lesser one.

Sailing for hats or competing for hardware.

Fishing for paltry perch or getting committed to catching souls.

The choice is yours—and mine—to make each day. Will we accept God's big-fish invitation?

Here's my vote: together, let's all echo the words that young Samuel cried to God one sleepless night so many years ago: "Speak, Lord! Your servant is listening." Tell God the truth about your desire to live out the abundance he has promised you: "As you direct, I will take action in the world around me. I'm going to live every single aspect of today with a Grander Vision! I will work with a Grander Vision. I will read with a Grander Vision. I will stand in lines with a Grander Vision. I will change diapers with a Grander Vision. I will drive my car with a Grander Vision. I will work out with a Grander Vision. I will cook dinner with a Grander Vision. I will vacation with a Grander Vision. I will pay taxes with a Grander Vision. And yes, as we explore another Luke 5 miracle in the next chapter, I will even party with a Grander Vision!

STUDY QUESTIONS

1. Think about the people you know at work, in your social life, at church, in your extended family, and so on. Do most people you know spend their lives for dollars or invest their lives for destinies?

2. If human nature says to chase the dollar, then why do you think Peter, James, and John were willing to follow Jesus and work to impact people's eternal destinies?

3. For Chuck Colson, choosing to live the Grander Vision meant radically shifting his priorities after being released from prison and investing in inmates' futures, both professionally and spiritually. In your particular situation, what would it look like for *you* to say yes to God's Grander Vision?

4. Reflecting back on the sailing analogy noted on pages 181–82, are there aspects of your life where you're still opting for the "hats" instead of pursuing the "hardware"? What keeps you settling for less than God's best in your life?

5. How did you feel when you read the story of the speaker who labeled everything "Temporary" at the conference? Why do you suppose so many people assign permanent significance to things that will one day fade away?

6. Think of one aspect of your life that you will choose to see through Grander Vision Living lenses today (check out the last paragraph of this chapter for a few suggestions), and be prepared to view the world differently than ever before!

CHAPTER 10

Matthew's Deepest Desire

· · · · •

Dusk was finally giving way to nighttime as another long day came to a close. The sun began to fall into the western sky, and in the shadowy light, the men started to recount the afternoon's adventures. "What a day!" one of them said, incredulous. "We must have walked at least twenty-five miles...."

Thinking back on the details of their journey stimulated all sorts of animated dialogue about the situations they'd encountered. There was the conversation with the centurion. The woman who actually washed Jesus' feet with her hair and her expensive perfume. (The disciples had no idea *what* to make of that one.) The miraculous healing of the widow's son in Nain. (The guy was deader than a doornail, and then all of a sudden he was skipping down Main Street. The townspeople were shocked, to say the least.)

As was typical, the men had gone from town to town, healing people, teaching them, and engaging them in discussion about how to get freed up from sin-enslaved living. Just imagine the dinnertime conversations of these friends on the heels of days like these!

Matthew—also called Levi, and more recently called "a disciple," if he remembered correctly—was sitting by the campfire with the whole gang, including Jesus, just soaking up the richness of community and fellowship. During a lull in the conversation, I can just picture one of the wisecracks of the bunch starting off softly, then building to full voice with, "It oooonly takes a spark ...," as the men fall apart in groans and laughter.

Not surprisingly, Peter had made fish for dinner. He and his brother Andrew had expertly filleted and grilled the tender white meat, served their friends their masterful creation, then stood back as they waited for first bites to be swallowed. "Well?" they asked expectantly. Their famished buddies had grunted their satisfaction as they kept shoveling chunks of fish into their mouths.

The men all prop up against the large, smooth rocks surrounding them to relax after a dinner that seemed to linger forever. Philip pipes up as he takes a seat near the fire. "Hey, Andrew, nice work with the wrong turn today. Did you know that the *whole* crowd was following you? Should have paid attention to Jesus' blind leading the blind bit the other day...." His wry grin gives him away. Good-natured jabs continue to punctuate the conversation, knitting these guys together like brothers. Even to outsiders it would be obvious that things like love and compassion, unity and servant-mindedness are present here.

Matthew's thoughts drift away from his immediate environment as he stares at the familiar faces around the circle. The laughter. The stories. The candor. The camaraderie. *It doesn't get any better than this!* he thinks as he tries to find a category for the soul-level intimacy he's experiencing. For Matthew, the landscape of his present life is dreamlike because only weeks ago, the concept of Christian community was totally foreign to him. Tax collectors didn't typically hang out with the fanatics who followed Jewish rabbis around. But Matthew had bet on a long shot, hitching his wagon to Jesus' star. And what a ride it had been so far!

Still lost in his own thoughts, his eyes finally land on Jesus'. Matthew is quickly jolted back into the conversation at hand. "Well, Matthew?" Jesus asks, a knowing smile on his face. Matthew grins back at the Savior of the world. "Uh, sorry ... guess I was somewhere else. What'd you say?"

●　　●　　●　　●　　●

In those days. Jewish tax collectors were outcasts. Even the Jewish religious leaders thought they were ravenous betrayers because they were known for taking hard-earned money from their fellow countrymen in order to stuff Caesar's pockets. The tax-collecting system was more or less legalized robbery designed to give Roman citizens a free ride through life. And it was in the midst of this corrupt scheme that Matthew's personal life took a wild turn.

Luke 5:27 says that Jesus went out one day, saw a tax collector sitting at his tax booth—someone obviously outside the family of faith—and told the guy to "follow him." I'm sure Matthew's comrades thought he'd lost his mind. Why on earth would a successful businessman ditch his career and traipse after a homeless rabbi? But Matthew would soon discover what Jesus already knew: choosing the Grander Vision leads to wealth that the world only *wishes* it could offer.

"Follow me!" he said to a wide-eyed Matthew that afternoon. And in a flash, the unscrupulous tax collector left everything—including his open cash register—to pursue Christ. Not unlike his newfound friend Peter, Matthew found that walking away from his business meant parting with his identity and his comfortable routine, not to mention his financial security.

Typical tax collectors made their living working for wealthy entrepreneurs, who received a take on all taxes levied. Once the tax collectors' financial requirements were met, they were free to pocket the surplus. Doesn't take a genius to determine that the savviest swindler wins the day in that scenario. But Matthew was so utterly compelled by Christ's invitation that he sidestepped his corrupt practice and instead chose to walk in the footsteps of the one who said he accepted *all* men—including even tax collectors, it seemed.

In my estimation, this wasn't the first time Matthew had laid eyes on Jesus. I think he had witnessed Jesus preach sermons and perform miracles during the days leading up to his conversion. But once he was face-to-face with the redeemer of the world, Matthew somehow discovered that with God, the crooked really *can* be made straight.

STAYING FRIENDS WITH SINNERS

For weeks, Matthew had traveled around with the other eleven disciples, helping Jesus accomplish his kingdom work. On one occasion, Jesus was teaching a group of people when Matthew looked out at the crowd and recognized several of his old tax-collecting buddies. *I wonder what they think about all of this*, he'd thought at the time.

And back at the campfire, those faces flashed like snapshots in his mind's eye. *Did they see me standing beside Jesus as he taught? Do they know that I'm on his side now?* The more he pondered it all, the more his questions plagued him. Here was Matthew, having just experienced the comfort and wonder and beauty of his very own Circle of Comfort, when a haunting reality overtook him. *I'm experiencing something truly amazing here tonight*, he thought. *And in addition to this astounding group of friends I now get to relate with, I have the assurance that once my time on earth here ends, I'm going to spend the rest of eternity in heaven. That's great news! But what in the world am I supposed to do about my tax-gathering buddies? They have no clue what my new life is all about....*

Matthew feels paralyzed as he wrestles with how he will explain to his old-life friends what his new life entails. What can he possibly say or do to provide some sort of bridge to keep his worlds from colliding? His wheels start spinning as those snapshots whiz through his mind like a video being watched in fast-forward mode. One by one, he focuses on the guys he's lived most of his young life with ... the same guys who as of yet have no hope of heaven.

Bartholomew gets up to stoke the fire as Matthew decides on a plan. "What if I throw a party?" he mutters to himself. "I mean, I *know* how to throw a party; my reputation proves it! What if I throw a party and I bring buddies from my old life and people from my new life to the same house, even stick them in the same room. And what if the people in my new life don't just hang around with each other but instead disperse and walk across my living room, rubbing shoulders with my old friends and opening themselves up to the activity of the Holy Spirit?"

By now, a few of the disciples overhear their friend, who is obviously deep in conversation ... with himself. But Matthew is undeterred. "Yeah," he continues, "what if my new friends are willing to step into the Zone of the Unknown [I'm sure they had those back then], and what if some spiritual sparks get ignited, and what if a half dozen of my buddies wind up in the kingdom like I did, all because of this one party? If *that* were to happen, it would be unbelievable!"

Stumbling over Peter and James and John, Matthew darts around the fire pit to sell Jesus on the idea. "What do you think, Lord?" Matthew asks with pleading eyes. Jesus doesn't hesitate. Not only does he agree that it's a great plan, but he also says that he'll come.

And in the days that follow, all of Matthew's friends consent to coming too—old and new, not-yet-saved and fully devoted believers alike.

·   ·   ·   ·   •

The night finally arrives, and things unfold exactly as Matthew had dreamed.
At *his* house, in *his* living room on that warm night, people from his old
life and people from his new life began mixing and talking, bumping up
against each other, just seeing if any sparks might fly. And can't you just
imagine Matthew standing over by the punch bowl at one point begging
God, "Please, please make something happen here tonight. Do something
radical in the hearts of my old buddies — just like you did in my own
heart!"

As Matthew is making an appeal for supernatural intervention, things
unfortunately take a dramatic turn. The Pharisees show up, miffed because
the invitation list appears to be way too broad. Matthew looks a little
stunned as the legalistic killjoys gripe at Jesus, who has some harsh words
for them in return. "You don't get it, do you! My Father is not *annoyed* or
put off by people who are outside of the family of God. He is wide open
to and, in fact, drawn *toward* those who need help the most. Like a doctor
who is walking around with a cure for some dreadful disease, he seeks out
people with the illness!"

Jesus perseveres, continuing to explain the heart of the Father to the
religious leaders this night, who never quite seem to get it. To them, Matthew's little gathering has suspicion written all over it — I mean, how can
it be an evangelistic event when everyone is having so much fun! All their
narrow-mindedness tells them is that Jesus has resorted to mingling with
social derelicts.

And at face value, it was true: Jesus was hanging out with career sinners. But the crux of his mission demanded it. Why? Because his nature
was to be more concerned about where people were headed than with
where they were when he found them, remember? He had come to redeem
sick sinners and quench thirsty souls, and he gladly stayed in the fray to
serve the agenda of a God who gave everything he had so that people just
like Matthew and his buddies could be restored.

·   ·   ·   ·   •

The power of Matthew's story gets me every time. One guy who is committed
to selfish living is unexpectedly invited to join God's family. His response
is to leave *everything* and immediately begin living a new life. As he gets

to know Jesus over time, he's utterly enamored by him. On top of that, he develops friendships with Peter and James and John, no doubt overdosing on joyous Christian fellowship. In short, he finds this new little community of men and women to be the best thing he has ever experienced.

There's just one problem. What's he going to do about his former friends? He can either hole away and ditch his old-life buddies, or he can choose to live the Grander Vision by getting all over the work of bridging the gap.

When he was first struck by the eternal realities facing his far-from-God friends, Matthew could have panicked and given up altogether. "I'm stuck, God. Frankly, I think it's best for all of us if I just walk away and let fate take its course with those guys."

But he didn't. Fortunately, with eternity hanging in the balance for them, Matthew faithfully found a way to get his friends introduced to the living Christ.

And I imagine that after the religious brass cleared out that night, Jesus threw his arm over Matthew's shoulder and said, "Matthew, I'm proud of you. You stuck your neck out there to throw this party, and I for one think it was a good idea. You were honest about who you are and what you're capable of doing. You knew the evangelistic options that would shut down your friends and which ones would light them up. You got creative and took risks, and I applaud you for that."

THE LEGACY OF MATTHEW PARTIES

Back in the early days of Willow, we talked with such frequency about the "Matthew Party" story in Luke 5 that it became part of the fabric of our church culture. Operating with Matthew's intuition for discerning next steps in the lives of seekers became sort of a way of life, and lots of us started throwing Matthew Parties, for want of a better name. They weren't part of a formal, programmatic effort. They were just casual ways to help people who were outside the family of God to get inside the family of God. Willow folks would grab a few people from the office and a few people from church and host a backyard barbeque or a pool party or hang out shooting pool in someone's basement. During the eighties and nineties, we heard of scores of people coming to faith as a result of these parties.

Over time, my desire to reflect Matthew's remarkable courage kept increasing. I got addicted to sticking my neck out there just as he did, pulling believers and nonbelievers into the same room and trusting God with the results. After a while, although the larger-scale buzz at Willow died down, I was one of those eternal optimists who never stopped believing in the power of the party. I never stopped seeking ways to gather some new-life friends together with some old-life friends just to see what might transpire. I never stopped rejoicing over that particular work of the Holy Spirit in my life, who used the simplicity of throwing a party to craft me into the type of person who better reflects the heart of the Father.

⁂ ⁂ ⁂ ⁂ ●

At Christmastime last year, I did what I have done every year following Willow's Christmas Eve service: I threw a Matthew Party. Despite wall-to-wall meetings, planning sessions, and run-throughs that week, my mind kept drifting to the Matthew Party that was only days away. I couldn't wait!

I had invited about twenty people who were living *extremely* far from God, by their own admission. These men and women had never been to Willow before, had never been to my house before, and spiritually speaking would profess to be "going it alone."

To that group, I added about twenty people who were in the Seeker Slow Lane—the remedial class of Christianity, you might say. On the rare occasion when I would badger them mercilessly, they'd agree to come to Willow. But it was sporadic attendance at best, usually involving a fair amount of kicking and screaming on their part. Most of them had been to my house previously to attend other parties, and all of them knew I was "working" on them, nudging them along the (very) slow path to God. Maybe they would step across the line of faith someday, but in my estimation, it was going to take some time. A *lot* of time.

In addition to the twenty or so people who were very far from God, and the twenty or so people who were in-progress types, I had sprinkled in a dozen or so very strong Christ-followers from Willow to mix it up a bit. The screening process for this group in particular had been intense! I knew I couldn't afford any overzealous types showing up. No truth vigilantes. No bounty hunters. Just normal, mature, relationally intelligent, open-hearted, radically inclusive people who understood how high the stakes were that night—after all, I was going to put them in a room with friends of mine who, apart from a bona fide miracle, would spend eternity apart from God.

As with every other year, fifteen minutes before guests arrived, my heart started beating fast. I'm sure the tension I felt was completely natural —I had no way to control the outcome of the party, no way of knowing how the guests would interact, and no way to prepare for the exact conversations that would unfold and what God would choose to do as a result.

But I wouldn't have traded that anxiety for anything in the world! As I greeted the first guests to arrive, I braced for the adventure to come as a final burst of adrenaline exploded. *Here we go!*

·　·　·　·　●

I wish you could have been there to watch what unfolded that night. In my house in Barrington, Illinois, in the twenty-first century, we enjoyed an approximation of Matthew's first-century experience. It was incredible to witness so many God-moments in the making, not to mention it was just a heck of a party. The first time I glanced down at my watch, it was well past midnight, and guests ended up staying until two o'clock the next morning—and only left then because I kicked them out.

So what was it that gave it the buzz? What made it such a magical, edgy experience? I mulled over questions like those in the hours and days that followed. Want to know what I decided? The single greatest reason that the party was such a success was because the Christ-followers I'd invited from Willow did *exactly* what Christ wants all of his followers to do: they took a walk across the room.

When the Willow people had first arrived, they gathered in little Creeker circles, safely huddling together to talk about the weather, the Christmas Eve stage set, plans for the weekend, you name it. (They had to start somewhere, I guess.) But then, after about twenty minutes, it happened —and I was so proud of them when it did. One by one, they looked around the room and started excusing themselves from each other's company. "Well, I'm not going to stay in this circle all night," they would murmur as their minds raced. *I'm going to walk across the living room and stick out my hand and introduce myself to someone.*

"Excuse me," they would say, if with a complete lack of confidence. And then slowly they turned and walked. And how I related to the thoughts they had as they made those walks. I'd made hundreds of similar walks across rooms, and I knew how fast their hearts were beating, how dry their mouths were becoming, how curious they were about what would take place once they said, "Hi. My name is ..."

Every step of the way across my living room that night, each Christ-follower was thinking, *I have no idea how this is going to turn out. I don't know if this guy is going to want to talk to me. I don't know if that woman will want to engage in conversation with me. But you know what? I'm going to give it a shot. I'm going to pray every step of the way as I walk across this room, I'm going to introduce myself, and then I'm going to step back and just see if God does anything more.*

The discussions instantly began to light up. I was so grateful that the Spirit was opening doors! Everyone at the party had attended the Christmas Eve service together, and that shared experience provided the perfect conversational springboard. Some people talked about how they'd never been on the inside of a church before. (What an honor that Willow was their first experience!) Others admitted to just needing "more facts," and still others had recently purchased Rick Warren's book *The Purpose Driven Life*, intending to read it over the holidays.

As I meandered through the crowd that night, I thought about all of the requests I'd made of God in the days leading up to the party. "Oh, if this person and that person could get together and be in conversation with one another, that would be incredible!" Or "If only so-and-so and my other friend could chat, that would be so kinetic — they have so much in common." Sure enough, while I wandered around my own home that night, refilling drinks and making sure people had enough to eat, I would catch a glimpse of those exact pairings occurring. "God is good!" I whispered quietly. "God is so good!"

Thankfully, no Pharisee types showed up at my house that night to throw water on the delicate sparks that were flickering. I remember walking back into the kitchen with a feeling of soul-level satisfaction. It took hours before that buzz wore off! Finally, after I had given everyone the boot, I halfheartedly picked up the remaining dishes, grabbed stray glasses, and headed back into the kitchen, dazed by the significance of all that had happened.

Sometime just before daybreak, my mind still racing from the mystical aspects of the party, I thought to myself, *The whole thing comes down to nights just like this one. The future of the kingdom of God comes down to whether individual rank-and-file Christ-followers will do in their everyday lives what just happened in my home tonight!*

It really is true: the spread of the gospel—at least in today's reality —boils down to whether you and I will continue to seek creative ways to engage our friends, inviting them to explore the abundance of the Christ-following life and helping them choose eternity with God instead of settling for a terrible fate when this life is all said and done.

THE GOOD, THE BAD, THE UGLY

Since those early days at Willow, I have probably hosted hundreds of similar occasions, each time growing more amazed by the power of the Matthew Party. Whenever one rolls around, I have this thought: *What if, because of this simple party, one person says yes to Christ, leaves everything else behind, and totally sells out to the Grander Vision? It would all be worth it—the preparation, the stress, the risk—if just one person could get transformed tonight!*

But if I'm being honest here, I have to admit that although there are times when the parties are a smashing success—like the Christmas party I described—there are also times when they're a total flop. I remember nights when I'd be meandering through my home during a party, eavesdropping on conversations and checking on people's provisions, when all of a sudden I'd realize that things were not going well. Conversations were limited to sports and politics. Energy was low. You know the feeling when a party isn't really much of a party. . . .

But that's no reason to give up entirely. Because when things *do* work out, the implications are magnificent.

LIVING A LIFE THAT COUNTS

If there's one thing I want you to glean from Matthew's example, it's that you can do this! Even if you're reading this thinking, *I can't even remember the last time someone far from God was in my home for a social occasion,* I want you to soak this up: in the same spirit as Matthew had, you can choose today to gather a few old-life friends with a few new-life friends, trusting God to do something mystical and miraculous in your midst.

You can do this! You can plan a barbeque or a pool party or whatever suits your personality and your situation. You can keep reminding yourself that Matthew had no specialized training or superior gifting that qualified him. He was just a guy who cared about his lost buddies and refused to sit around while they frittered away their lives.

Matthew Parties don't have to be formal, expensive, elaborate, or perfectly orchestrated. They just have to *happen*. Remember the seeker-and-stray dinners I attend each week? There's nothing special about them, other than the fact that Christ-followers and people far from God have a safe, consistent opportunity to do life together. The host for these dinners is my good friend Jim Glas. Jim's spiritual journey has been marked by disillusionment from the time of his youth, but he remains committed to giving every member of our group a seat at the dining room table, several sets of listening ears, and an open forum for talking about whatever needs to be talked about.

When you're faithful to set up an environment like that, I believe Christ says the same thing to us today that he said to Matthew back then. "Thank you for caring for me by caring for my people. Thank you for using the gifts I've given you—your creativity and personality and access to resources—to engage your friends in the process of knowing me! Way to go!"

STUDY QUESTIONS

1. Why do you suppose Jesus chose ordinary fishermen and corrupt tax collectors as disciples rather than handpicking people who were a bit more cultured and holy?

2. What types of things did you give up in order to follow Jesus? Has it been worth it? Why or why not?

3. Matthew—a former tax collector himself—was probably keenly aware that his former business associates would think he was crazy to cash in his entire career and follow Jesus instead. If Matthew were alive today and came to you for advice on how to deal with the raised eyebrows and cynical questions of his old friends, what would you say?

4. Despite the fact that Matthew had only been following Jesus for a short time when he decided to host his banquet, somehow he knew he could trust Jesus to be gracious and accepting of his close friends—most of whom were also corrupt tax collectors. Do you believe Jesus is still in the business of receiving people in this manner? Why or why not?

5. On pages 200–201, you read that no matter who you are, you too can do this—you too can host a Matthew Party and allow spiritual sparks to fly right in your own living room. Think creatively about the opportunity that is now in front of you. What type of Matthew Party would you have? Who would you invite, and what would you hope they would glean from the experience?

CHAPTER 11

Open Doors

· · · · ·

Ready for a "famous last words" quiz? See if you can guess who said each of the following things just before he died:

"I regret that I have but one life to lose for my country."

"Now ... the mystery."

"Et tu, Brute?"

"I still live."

"I want to go, God ... take me."

"Please! Leave the shower curtain on the inside of the tub!"

All right, let's see how you fared. Here are the six mystery men revealed: Nathan Hale, Henry Ward Beecher, Julius Caesar, Daniel Webster, Dwight D. Eisenhower, and Conrad Hilton, founder of Hilton Hotels in the early 1900s. (I happened to stay in a Hilton last week and saw a plaque with those exact words hanging on the bathroom wall. But I digress.)

A person's last words mean something, don't they? Occasionally they are funny, like Hilton's. But usually they are poignant and heartfelt. Most times, a person's last words express the deepest convictions of the heart. It's like they're saying, "Here's the main thought I want to be remembered for. . . ."

For the last two chapters, we've been looking at what it means to choose Grander Vision Living over other, less-fulfilling options. And if I could point you to a single passage of Scripture to help you wrap your mind and heart around what it means to fully embrace this type of life, I'd pick a five-verse segment from the book of Colossians.

Near the beginning of Colossians chapter 4, Paul wraps up a letter that was painstakingly written to the church at Colossae from a dark, isolated prison cell. And if you study this letter long enough, you realize that this particular section of text represents the final substantive content from Paul to the Colossian church. The rest of the letter involves final greetings and personal matters—the kind of stuff many of us would put in a "PS." So in essence, as far as the believers at Colossae were concerned, these were Paul's "famous last words." Here is what he said:

> *Devote yourselves to prayer, being watchful and thankful. And pray for us, too, that God may open a door for our message, so that we may proclaim the mystery of Christ, for which I am in chains. Pray that I may proclaim it clearly, as I should. Be wise in the way you act toward outsiders; make the most of every opportunity. Let your conversation be always full of grace, seasoned with salt, so that you may know how to answer everyone.*[10]

Paul's burning desires for the people in Colossae were that they would stay rooted in Christ. That they would continue in their faith. That they wouldn't be deceived by the world's enticing ideas. And finally, that they would let peace rule in their lives. But when forced to put pen to paper in introducing these big ideas, he summed up his thoughts this way: "Devote yourselves to prayer."

In case you wonder exactly what Paul meant by that statement, you'll be pleased to know that I piled up all of my study aids on my desk and took time to really dig into this text. I offer my findings below regarding precisely what this phrase means. Ready for what I discovered?

Devote. Yourselves. To prayer. (That's it.)

It means pray, and pray a lot! Pray when you're alone. Pray when you're with a lot of people. Pray when you're in small groups. Pray on your way in; pray on your way out. Pray in your closet, in your car, at your desk. Pray morning prayers, pray mealtime prayers, pray in between mealtimes. Pray fervently, expectantly, and unself-consciously. Pray when you're burdened, worried, sick, or brokenhearted. Pray when you're soaring, setting records, or dancing on a mountaintop. Pray when you're up, and pray when you're down. Pray when you're healthy, when you're sick, when you feel like it, and when you don't. (*Especially* when you don't.)

Pray when you're busy; pray when you're bored. Pray before the big game, during it, and after it. In short, pray! And do so with devotedness.

Dallas Willard says that the more we pray, the more we *think* to pray.[11] In other words, the frequency with which we pray begins to build a kind of momentum like what Paul describes in 1 Thessalonians 5:16, where he encourages Christ-followers to "pray continually," or to "pray without ceasing," as another translation says.

When I was a young believer, that concept boggled my mind. Praying without ceasing—was Paul serious? Was it really possible? It defied my understanding.

But some of you who have devoted yourselves to prayer, stretching yourselves over the years to persevere in dialogue with God, know that it really is possible. For you, ongoing prayer is like breathing, and to shut it off in your world would be like sending a diver down without a tank.

Interestingly, in the short space of five verses, Paul gives away the secret to effective evangelism: if you ever hope to lead people to Christ, you have to be a person devoted to prayer. Prayer and effective evangelism, effective evangelism and prayer—the two are inextricably bound up. And in his final instructions to the Colossians, he essentially says, "Don't even think about doing the work of evangelism until you're all prayed up!"

His words apply to us today as well. And if we're serious about pointing our friends and family members toward God, we'd first better figure out how to put some wind in the sails of our prayer lives.

CATCH PRAYERS

One of the guys I had a hand in leading to Christ a few years back cornered me one day about the pray-without-ceasing thing. "What's it all about?" he asked. "Is it really doable?" His questions were reminiscent of the skepticism I had dealt with decades before.

I searched for an analogy that would shed some light on things. "Okay, try to think of it this way," I said. "Here at Willow, part of our staff phone system includes a 'Do Not Disturb' feature. If staff members are in meetings, brainstorming sessions, or sensitive counseling situations and need a few minutes of uninterrupted time, then they can push the Do Not Disturb button and have peace and quiet for as long as it's activated.

"But every once in a while, after their time of dedicated focus is over, staff members forget that the feature is on and go for *days* without anybody being able to communicate with them." (It's one of my special joys in ministry to track these wonderful folks down and ... pray with them!)

"Here's the point," I continued. "These particular people never seemed concerned in the least that they'd gone hours, sometimes days, with no incoming communication whatsoever. Didn't faze them one bit!

"With that image in mind, now contrast it with the staff and volunteers who work in our reception area. They are so intensely concerned about communicating with people that they actually wear *headsets*. Morning, noon, or night, those headsets are perched on top of their heads, ready to facilitate the process of them receiving information. Frankly, the worst possible thing in their world would be if internal communication ceased for even a moment. They are that devoted to carrying on the conversation."

I summed it up this way: "When you understand the concept of being devoted to prayer, it's as if you have one ear tuned in to the conversation you're in, while the other ear is tuned in to God. You may be in dialogue with someone about any number of things—the latest news or sports or how work is going, whatever—but you are constantly asking, *God, is this an open door? Do you want me to probe that? Do you want me to encourage him? What do you need or want me to do? Guide me here, please.*"

. . . . . •

Maybe you've experienced the dynamic of driving or working while simultaneously carrying on a conversation with God. Part of your brain is wrapped around the day's challenges, but another part is telling God, "I know there's a lot going on, but I know I won't face any of it alone. Thank you, God, for being with me and for giving me power and wisdom."

You might walk into a room for a meeting, and while you are engaging and concentrating on the tasks at hand, you ask God, "We're engaged in this business endeavor, concentrating on the tasks at hand, but are we on the right path? Steer us according to your plans, not ours. Help me know whether I'm handling myself in a constructive way in this meeting or if I'm misbehaving."

CLOSET PRAYERS

In Matthew 6:6—the Sermon on the Mount passage—Jesus teaches that in addition to offering ongoing "catch prayers" to God, there are occasions when you should go into your room, shut the door, and pray alone. These are intended to be times of more formalized and unrushed prayer when deep confession of sin can occur, followed by intimate times with God as he inspires and corrects, teaches and soothes you. They're what I call "closet prayers"—and they are equally essential to the vibrancy of a person's prayer life.

When I'm not on the road, I have a practice of getting to my office in Barrington early in the morning, shutting the doors, and spending twenty or thirty minutes in a more formal posture of prayer. I pray for the people I know I'll meet with that day. I pray over my agenda, asking for God's wisdom in investing each hour of that day wisely. I pray for staff issues and organizational issues and vision issues related to my responsibilities at Willow, asking God for his guidance and leadership in my life and ministry. These "closet prayer" experiences are always powerful times of recalibrating my world to God's world.

I tend to exhibit a "driver" personality, and so a little phrase I began carrying around with me is this: "When I work, I work. But when I pray, *God* works." It helps me remember that when I pray, the God of the entire universe works on my behalf, and *his* is a kind of work that moves us all upfield.

If you were to assess your own patterns, which do you need more of, closet prayers or catch prayers? Most of us are better at practicing one or the other—my challenge to you is that you hone your skills in *both* so that we can all be fully devoted pray-ers before God.

WHAT TO PRAY FOR

Paul continues in Colossians 4 by expounding on his burning desire for that church—and for us. The spirit of his comments is this: "Please pray for us, because we're striving night and day to *make Christ known* to those who are far from God." And what follows in verses 3–6 are some of the most wonderful phrases in all of Scripture related to your friends and family members coming to Christ:

> *Pray for us, too, that God may open a door for our message, so that we may proclaim the mystery of Christ, for which I am in chains. Pray that I may proclaim it clearly, as I should. Be wise in the way you act toward*

outsiders; make the most of every opportunity. Let your conversation be always full of grace, seasoned with salt, so that you may know how to answer everyone.

I love the nugget tucked away in verse 3. "Pray for us that God may open a door for our message," Paul says. He's no longer new to the evangelism thing. He's been spreading the word and taking his beatings for some time now, and as he nears the end of his life and his service to God, it's no coincidence that his final plea is that his spiritual brothers and sisters pray for open doors. Why? Because Paul had learned that you simply cannot *force* people to receive the message. You can't cram Christ through closed doors!

So he says in essence, "Pray for open doors of receptivity in people's minds and hearts, because without that, we're sunk." The same sentiment is echoed by another apostle in John 6:44, which says essentially, "No one comes to faith unless they are first drawn by the activity (or initiative) of God."

•   •   •   •   •

Some of you may know that a few years back I started a rather silly spiritual discipline in order to balance the activist side of my personality. The commitment was this: each morning, the first part of my body to hit the floor would, without fail, be my knees. This may sound easy, but I dare you to try it. It takes a little finagling to get your hips and legs to swing just right so that your knees come down before your feet. Before making that commitment, I had learned that if my feet hit the floor first, I was off to the races. Without giving God as much as a "Good morning," I would rush through my shower, jump into the car, and immediately get dialed in for the workday ahead. I was so driven that God simply couldn't keep up. (Relax, I'm kidding.)

So to right my Type-A tendencies, I decided to roll out of bed each day and, as a representation of my submitted spirit and will and attitude, adopt a posture of prayer. It's of symbolic import to me because it sends a message to me and to all of heaven that I'm in this thing—this life, this ministry, this day—*soli Deo gloria*, for God's glory.

Then, with my knees on the floor and my elbows on the side of the bed, I start by murmuring prayers of adoration and confession, of thanksgiving and submission. Then I pray for open doors: "God, would you open doors for me today—doors of conversation where I can say a word for you; doors of new relationships that may one day lead to spiritual conversations; doors of first encounters with people living far from you that may one day lead to solid relationships? Please go before me today, swinging them wide open so that I can walk in your activity!"

You know what? God *loves* to hear this prayer coming from his kids! He gets an enormous kick out of swinging doors open and then watching us stand there in awe each time. *Where'd* that *come from?* we think after a "coincidental" experience, while someone in heaven is smiling broadly.

In previous chapters, I've mentioned how important it is to watch for "open doors" in your interactions with people. And you wouldn't believe the corresponding ratio between the number of times I pray for an open door and the number of times God swings one loose.

Uncanny.

* * * * ●

On a recent trip to Europe, I got up one morning and was instantly greeted by the realization that I'd be facing a lot of complex issues that day. More than being concerned about the content of the talks I was scheduled to give, I felt burdened by how to overcome several language barriers, how I would deal with the always-interesting French/American dynamic, and how I would stay attuned to the Spirit's promptings in the midst of distractions. So I got on my knees and prayed. Before I finished the prayer, I added, "God, if you would open the door of conversation with somebody today, I'd be happy to walk right through...."

An hour later, as I waited in the hotel lobby for my ride, the night watchman was standing by a far counter, glancing alternatively at the morning paper and at me. We struck up a relatively safe conversation, and for some reason I felt the freedom to ask him about his accent. "You have an accent that sure doesn't seem French to me—where'd you grow up?"

"A place you Americans have never heard of," came the response.

"Hey, try me!"

He grinned a grin that said, *I told you so!* then said, "Tunisia."

Not easily dissuaded, I took a risk. "You didn't grow up in *Hammamet*, did you?" I'd been to Tunisia a grand total of one time and got lost one day, somehow landing in Hammamet.

His neck jerked back, his eyebrows raised up, and he looked at me as if I were a prophet. He was floored! Probably thought I had a crystal ball in my briefcase. Before he got too tangled up in his questions, I explained to him how I'd landed in some Tunisian city, got lost driving around, ended up in Hammamet, and so on. It was the only city I knew to say, I confessed.

"What are you doing in Paris?" he asked, still stunned that I'd heard of his hometown.

"Actually, I'm here to help pastors spread the love of Christ to average people walking the streets of Paris."

His answer is still fresh on my mind. "I've never met them," he said, "these pastors who care about the average people walking Paris's streets."

"Well, that's what I'm here to do," I said with as much compassion as I could convey.

That brief exchange led to a very interesting conversation about the nuances of Islam and Christianity. He gave me his card as my ride pulled up, and upon returning to the States, I followed up with him to see if we could continue the conversation that was begun in the lobby of a French hotel that day.

As I prayed that night, I said with a smile and characteristic disbelief, "I mean, really, God, you opened a door with a guy from Hammamet! How does *that* happen?!"

· · · · •

On another occasion, I agreed to speak at a pastors' meeting down south and could only make it work by chartering a flight in and out of the location. Upon landing, I wound up on the wrong side of Palwaukee Airport. I spotted an older woman standing just outside the small terminal and asked for her help.

"I think you want to be waaay over there," she said as she extended her arm, her thick index finger pointing in the opposite direction. "But guess what! I'm headed over there now! Hop in; I'll take you. Where are you headed to, anyway?"

"San Antonio," I replied as I eased into the backseat. She told me energetically that she had done military training in San Antonio.

Well, that sparked absolutely nothing in my tired brain. I took a stab. "Uh, how did that go?" I asked.

"Heh," she sort of laughed. "I barely *remember* the entire decade of the seventies. Pills, booze, the whole bit. Hardly remember a thing, ya know?"

I was stumped again. "So how did the eighties go?" I ventured.

"Equally blurry."

Despite fearing her response, I kept going. "And the nineties?"

"Not as bad, but not great," she said with a satisfied nod.

"But then at the turn of millennium," I laughed, "you probably found God and started teaching Sunday school, right?"

She tossed her head over her right shoulder and just shook it back and forth. "Uh, *no*! That didn't happen at all!" She may as well have added, "You loon!"

"Well, I was just hoping," I said with a smile.

"You know, I didn't ask you before, but why are you going to San Antonio?"

I was grateful for the gear shift. "I train pastors. And I'm training pastors in San Antonio." She didn't immediately fill the pause, so I continued. "Do you have any sort of spiritual background at all?"

"Hon, I number myself among the *permanently* religiously challenged," she said.

"Well, you won't believe this," I said, "but the pastors I'm teaching are trying to *reach* the permanently religiously challenged."

"Get outta here!" she said playfully. She gave a belly laugh that I won't soon forget, and as we pulled up to my destination, I hopped out of the car, reached my arm through the open passenger side window, and shook her hand.

Catching her eye, I said, "Really, there are a lot of us who care deeply for the permanently religiously challenged—people just like you. And my guess is that there are some really good reasons you're that way. Maybe you ought to give God another chance." She glanced out the windshield and then toward me, smiling in response to how tenderly our brief conversation had ended.

*   *   *   *   •

When God chooses to open a door, amazing opportunities unfold. I join arms with the apostle Paul in exhorting you: "Every day, pray for open doors.

Because unless God goes before you, makes the way, softens a heart, readies a spirit, you will get absolutely nowhere."

Imagine what would happen if every single morning every one of us prayed fervently that God would open doors for us that day!

But Paul doesn't stop at praying for open doors. He also prays for all that will unfold after he steps through that open door. Colossians 4:4 says, "Pray that I may proclaim it clearly, as I should." In other words, Paul says, "If God should open the door, then more than anything else, pray that I will make the message clear!" Don't miss the most fascinating aspect of his request: Paul doesn't request prayers for him to be clever or likable or impressive. Just clear.

Some of you fully understand the intensity with which Paul makes his request. You've experienced the sensation of seeing a door fly open while you stand there thinking, *Batter up! This is it!* In that moment, you know you've got one shot. And like Paul you think, *Oh, God, please help me to be clear!*

WHEN YOU SEE A DOOR OPEN, WALK THROUGH!

Paul goes on, encouraging us all to be wise in the way we act toward outsiders. I love this about Paul. He's at the stage in his life where he has seen evangelism done in such poor, counterproductive, and pitiful ways that he starts pleading with folks: "Look, we can't bust these doors open—only God can do that. But once he does, we've just *got* to make the message clear to people! Please hear me: you must stop doing damage to the cause! Stop acting unwisely toward unbelievers. Toss out any obnoxious, overzealous, superiority-clad verbiage and actions that push people away! Just—be—*wise.* Be emotionally and relationally intelligent. Be sensitive. Pray and listen before you preach. Exercise great care when you tell your story, when you tell God's story.

"Here's how I'd like to see it done," Paul continues. "For starters, I'd like your conversation to be full of grace. *Filled* with grace—what a fantastic goal! In essence, what Paul is asking is that our conversations with outsiders be *simultaneously* loving, winsome, and grace-filled.

·   ·   ·   ·   •

On the trip to Europe I mentioned previously, a group of friends and I spent a few days on a boat sailing around different islands in the Adriatic Sea. While docked one morning, several of us decided to go for a walk to get some exercise and happened upon a thousand-year-old church that had a large graveyard behind it. We wandered around scores of gravestones, three unbelievers and me, just taking in names and dates and epitaphs.

One of the guys pointed to a particular grave and said, "Hey, that guy's probably in purgatory. Probably didn't pay his penance, you know, and has been in limbo for the past two hundred years! You're the professional here, Hybels. Why don't you explain all this purgatory stuff to us? I mean, what's the deal with the whole penance thing? Just tell the rest of us what it's all about."

Call me crazy, but it seemed like an open door to me. They all stared at me, nodding. "Yeah, tell us!" they ribbed.

My mind whirred. *I've got about forty-five seconds to make something clear here. Where should I begin?*

I live for moments like those! Why? Because I have absolutely no idea what's going to come out of my mouth in response. But I trust that God's going to direct some logical flow and make it all work out. Each time, I echo Paul's words, "Oh, God, please make this clear!"

This probably isn't what I said verbatim, but something like this rolled off my tongue as the four of us stood in a deserted graveyard on a windy morning in May: "Well, for starters, I've never done an in-depth study on purgatory or the whole penance plan. I'm far from being an expert on those things, but this much I know for sure: the Bible teaches that God is utterly *heartbroken* when anybody ends up anywhere but with him eternally in heaven. And he sent Christ, his Son, to pay everybody's penance so that we wouldn't have to. When we ask him personally to pay our penance, Jesus joyfully agrees to do so, and that opens the door for that person to be in heaven with God forever."

Surprisingly, as I finished my remarks, there was no applause.

There were no follow-up questions, no falling-on-knees-in-submission-to-Christ motions. Just a simple, "So that's the deal, huh?" from one of them. And a bunch of stares. (Although later that day, one of them did cycle back around for what turned out to be a fantastic spiritual conversation.)

Based on the situation and on my time constraints, I'm really not sure my response was the best possible one I could have offered. But it was the one I came up with, and I trust God with the results. Regardless of whether you would have chosen the words I chose in response to my friend's question, there is at least some method to my madness that informed what I said. When I'm in a conversation that begins to turn spiritual and want to say a word for God, there are only three things I focus on. Doesn't matter which framework I'm using—it could be the good deeds / bad deeds scale, the bridge drawing, the "do versus done" explanation, or any number of other illustrations that are appropriate to the situation—there are still only three core ideas I have to make sure I convey. I call them "irreducible ingredients."

IRREDUCIBLE INGREDIENT #1:
GOD LOVES YOU

The first thing I do to ensure that my message is crystal clear is to communicate this truth: "Our God is filled with love and compassion no matter who's dug what kind of hole for themselves, no matter how far they've drifted away. God loves you!"

In the graveyard that morning, I knew it would be ineffectual to argue purgatory versus heaven and hell. But I did want to make one thing clear: God is heartbroken anytime anybody doesn't wind up in heaven. In Matthew 18:14 Christ himself says, "In the same way your Father in heaven is not willing that any of [his children] should perish." I wanted them to know that God's arms are open for any and all!

IRREDUCIBLE INGREDIENT #2:
CHRIST CHOSE TO PAY FOR YOU

The second important idea to communicate is that no amount of human effort can ever make someone "right" with God. The theological term for this idea is *substitutionary atonement*, meaning that Christ did for human beings what they could not do for themselves.

Based on my experience, if you were to line up a hundred people, ninety-nine of them would say that if they're ever going to be made right with God, they'll have to do it themselves. Culturally, it's counterintuitive to consider that Christ has already built that bridge we talked about in chapter 7. In our independence-junky society, most people just can't accept that they can't save themselves. Which is why in the cemetery, I said it's not about penance-paying. The key thing I needed them to understand was that the debt they owed was already paid in full.

IRREDUCIBLE INGREDIENT #3:
THE CHOICE IS NOW YOURS

The third clear message to convey is this: there is a decision to be made regarding the first two ideas. A person will never, ever *drift* into salvation. No, a person must opt into or opt out of Christ's plan of salvation. For this reason, I told my three buddies that morning that once someone asks (decision point) Christ to pay his penance, Christ joyfully does so!

Again, there are countless ways to convey these three messages, many of which we've surfaced in previous chapters. Whatever presentation you choose, be sure to make them clear:

- God loves every person he created—including you!
- Christ does for you what nobody can do for him- or herself.
- At some point, you have to make a decision about it.

       ◦   ◦   ◦   ◦   ●

Let me come back to something Paul requested in verse 6—the one about conversations with outsiders being seasoned with salt. I can remember several occasions when I've been in a sensitive conversation and have said something to the effect of, "You know, what we're talking about here is the single most important thing you can be wrapping your brain around. This is your eternity, your forever, your everything! If we need to spend a few extra minutes to get this just right, let's take the time. It's that important!"

Or sometimes I'll say, "If you wake up in the middle of the night thinking about this stuff, pay attention. It's worth losing a night's sleep over your eternity!"

These are "salty" comments, or "edge" as I call it. In your efforts to be graceful, don't neglect to call a spade a spade. As I explained a couple of chapters ago, Jesus lived and breathed with a high degree of urgency regarding eternal matters.

One of the all-time masters at striking this balance is Billy Graham. Time and again he teaches a clear message. He prays that God will open doors. He treats seekers with incredible integrity and sensitivity. Then he comes to the invitation and says, "There is room at the cross for *you*, just as you are. And now is the time for you to take a stand! A decision has to be made. Get up out of your seat today, because there are no guarantees about tomorrow. The most important decision of your life is this one. Choose well!"

Friends, we have to get this right. We have to pray for open doors. We must make the message clear. We should aim for being attractive to outsiders. We need to be full of grace while being faithful to add edge. And then we can joyously leave it all in God's capable hands.

THE GOAL OF THE WALK-ACROSS-THE-ROOM PERSON

I have seen firsthand what happens to human lives when Christ takes his rightful place in the heart of an individual. In the home of a family. In the heart of a church. In the seat of a community. The ripple effect of faith is astounding! And do you know where your ripple effect begins? With you walking across a room. Telling a straightforward story. Drawing a simple picture. Pointing people toward God. That's where it all begins. And you can do this! You can be the spiritual adrenaline injection for your sphere of influence.

In preparation for our annual elders' retreat one summer, one of our elders secretly went around asking people whose personal lives had been touched by the other elders to write a note of thanks to them, which she then framed and presented as gifts to each one of us. To this day I have no idea how she pulled it off, but somehow she tracked down an old sailing crew buddy of mine, the infamous Dave Wright.

Dave's journey to faith was anything but a straight line, but the day finally arrived when he made a powerful decision to begin following Christ—a decision that transformed every nook and cranny of his heart, soul, and life. Talk about a spiritual adrenaline injection for all of us who call ourselves his friends! To this day, he is known by most as "Super

Dave," a well-suited moniker for a man with the most expansive heart you'll find. These days, his life influences hundreds of thousands of people as he faithfully serves the Willow Creek Association.

The words he penned in response to the elder's request for the note will stick with me until my dying day. You can read it for yourself—here's the letter that is now framed in my office area.

> 7/18/99
> Bill:
>
> I am a Christian! I owe this to you and God. I am so thankful that you listened when he prompted you to start a sailing team of non-Christians. I sincerely and deeply appreciate your never-ending patience and guidance over the past eight years. Our friendship is priceless to me, and I love you.
> For eternity,
> Super

Those of you who have known someone on both sides of their faith commitment understand that no trophy, no promotion, no pleasure, no possession will ever hold a candle to the thrill we feel when God uses us to touch another human life for eternity.

·　·　·　·　•

At some point, if you are a follower of Christ's, you're going to say your final farewell to this planet and head to heaven for all eternity. When you get there, you'll meet several of my sailing buddies, neighbors, and friends. You'll meet a woman who stood thirsty beside a well one afternoon but who had her eternal thirst quenched by the Living Water himself. You'll meet a man who was bound to a wheelchair while on earth but who today is playing catch on the streets of heaven. You'll meet a guy named Peter who will probably be wearing a "Fish Big or Go Home" T-shirt. Depending on when you get there, you'll meet a city councilman from Illinois and a former aid to President Nixon, both of whom realized that kingdom power trumps political power any day. You'll meet people who were once lost but somehow got found. People who were chasing dollars but learned they could have a hand in pointing friends and family members toward an eternal destiny with God.

And who could forget Matthew? Surely you'll be eager to meet the former tax collector who experienced mind-boggling, in-person adventures with Jesus Christ—as well as a few former tax-collecting friends who had their worlds rocked when the love of Christ invaded their hearts.

If you're like me, you'll probably walk right up to him and ask to hear his radical before-and-after story firsthand. And I just bet that as you approach Matthew, slowing a little because you notice that he's in the middle of a conversation, you'll be overjoyed to discover that the person he's talking to is your friend, your father, your neighbor, your boss, your teacher, your hairstylist, the owner of your dry-cleaning service.

This is unbelievable! you'll think as you take in the person standing in front of you. You can think of nothing else to ask but the one question that would be on anyone's mind when they find a career sinner on the right side of the pearly gates: "How'd you get here?!"

"You know, I was just a jumble of knots, so twisted up about this whole God-thing," the explanation will begin, "until the day when you walked across that room. *That* day—that was the day things started getting worked out for me."

STUDY QUESTIONS

1. What is your greatest take-away from this chapter?

2. Which do you find easier to maintain, the practice of "catch" praying—offering up ongoing bursts of communication with God— or the practice of "closet" praying—committing to times of intense, private dialogue with him? What might you stand to gain from honing your abilities in the other arena?

3. Part of Paul's request in Colossians 4 is for people to pray for open doors in his ministry. Have you ever seen God open a door right after you prayed for one? Describe your experience.

4. Another part of Paul's request deals with the manner in which the message would get conveyed. What do you think it means for a Christ-follower's speech to be "full of grace"?

5. Look over this chapter again and review the three evangelistic "irreducible ingredients." Why do you suppose the third ingredient is so critical to communicate to people who are living far from God?

6. As you reflect on the closing scene of this book, whose faces come to mind? Which of your unconvinced friends and family members are you hoping to bump into on the streets of heaven someday? How might your decision to become a walk-across-the-room person increase the likelihood of their eternal presence there?

Notes

1. 1997–2002 ©GlaxoSmithKline, citing American Podiatric Medical Association, www.apma.org.

2. Philippians 2:6–8.

3. Dr. Gilbert Bilezikian, *Christianity 101: Your Guide to Eight Basic Christian Beliefs* (copyright © Gilbert Bilezikian, 1993), 35.

4. Summary of statements from Garry Poole's *Seeker Small Groups*, p. 208.

5. Poole, Garry, *The Complete Book of Questions: 1001 Conversation Starters for Any Occasion* (South Barrington, Ill.: Willow Creek Association, 2003).

6. Luke 5:4.

7. Luke 23:34.

8. Romans 8:15–17a, 19–21 MSG.

9. Hebrews 9:27; Acts 4:12; Romans 6:23.

10. Colossians 4:2–6.

11. Dallas Willard, *The Spirit of the Disciplines: Understanding How God Changes Lives* (New York: HarperCollins, 1998), 185.

WILLOW
Willow Creek Association

Willow Creek Association
Vision, Training, Resources for Prevailing Churches

This resource was created to serve you and to help you build a local church that prevails. It is just one of many ministry tools that are part of the Willow Creek Resources® line, published by the Willow Creek Association together with Zondervan.

The Willow Creek Association (WCA) was created in 1992 to serve a rapidly growing number of churches from across the denominational spectrum that are committed to helping unchurched people become fully devoted followers of Christ. Membership in the WCA now numbers over 12,000 Member Churches worldwide from more than ninety denominations.

The Willow Creek Association links like-minded Christian leaders with each other and with strategic vision, training, and resources in order to help them build prevailing churches designed to reach their redemptive potential. Here are some of the ways the WCA does that.

- **The Leadership Summit**—a once a year, two-and-a-half-day conference to envision and equip Christians with leadership gifts and responsibilities. Presented live at Willow Creek as well as via satellite broadcast to over 130 locations across North America, this event is designed to increase the leadership effectiveness of pastors, ministry staff, volunteer church leaders, and Christians in the marketplace.

- **Ministry-Specific Conferences** — throughout each year the WCA hosts a variety of conferences and training events — both at Willow Creek's main campus and offsite, across the U.S., and around the world — targeting church leaders and volunteers in ministry-specific areas such as: small groups, preaching and teaching, the arts, children, students, volunteers, stewardship, etc.

- **Willow Creek Resources®** — provides churches with trusted and field-tested ministry resources in such areas as leadership, evangelism, spiritual formation, spiritual gifts, small groups, stewardship, student ministry, children's ministry, the use of the arts — drama, media, contemporary music — and more.

- **WCA Member Benefits** — includes substantial discounts to WCA training events, a 20 percent discount on all Willow Creek Resources®, *Defining Moments* monthly audio journal for leaders, quarterly *Willow* magazine, access to a Members-Only section on WillowNet, monthly communications, and more. Member Churches also receive special discounts and premier services through WCA's growing number of ministry partners — Select Service Providers — and save an average of $500 annually depending on the level of engagement.

For specific information about WCA conferences, resources, membership, and other ministry services contact:

Willow Creek Association
P.O. Box 3188
Barrington, IL 60011-3188
Phone: 847-570-9812
Fax: 847-765-5046
www.willowcreek.com

Share Your Thoughts

With the Author: Your comments will be forwarded to
the author when you send them to *zauthor@zondervan.com.*

With Zondervan: Submit your review of this book
by writing to *zreview@zondervan.com.*

Free Online Resources at
www.zondervan.com/hello

 Zondervan AuthorTracker: Be notified whenever your favorite authors publish new books, go on tour, or post an update about what's happening in their lives.

 Daily Bible Verses and Devotions: Enrich your life with daily Bible verses or devotions that help you start every morning focused on God.

 Free Email Publications: Sign up for newsletters on fiction, Christian living, church ministry, parenting, and more.

 Zondervan Bible Search: Find and compare Bible passages in a variety of translations at www.zondervanbiblesearch.com.

 Other Benefits: Register yourself to receive online benefits like coupons and special offers, or to participate in research.